FREE YOURSELF from DEPRESSION

By Michael D. Yapko, Ph.D.

Rodale Press, Emmaus, Pennsylvania

With the deepest love to my wife, Diane. I can't imagine a better partner to go through life with.

Notice

This book is intended as a reference volume only, not as a medical manual. It is not a substitute for any treatment that may have been prescribed by your doctor. If you suspect that you have a medical problem, we urge you to seek competent medical help.

Author's Note

The case examples presented in this book accurately represent clients I have worked with. The names have been changed, of course, to protect their privacy.

Printed in the United States of America on acid-free ∞, recycled paper ♲

Editor: Charles Gerras
Copy Editor: Ellen Pahl
Indexer: Andrea Chesman

Book Design by Ruttle, Shaw, and Wetherill, Inc.
Cover Design by Jerry O'Brien

If you have any questions or comments concerning this book, please write:
Rodale Press
Book Reader Service
33 E. Minor St.
Emmaus, PA 18098

Library of Congress Cataloging-in-Publication Data

Yapko, Michael D.
    Free yourself from depression / by Michael D. Yapko.
        p.   cm.
    Includes index.
    ISBN 0-87857-987-7 hardcover
    1. Depression, Mental—Popular works.   2. Depression, Mental—Treatment.   I. Title.
    RC537.Y35   1992
    616.85'27—dc20   91-27031
                                                             CIP

Distributed in the book trade by St. Martin's Press

2 4 6 8 10 9 7 5 3 1   hardcover

Contents

Acknowledgments

First and foremost, my heartfelt thanks go out to my clients. You are the ones who challenged me, pushed me, and gave me all the reasons to care. I have learned more lessons of life from you than I thought possible. You are wonderful teachers.

I want to thank my wife, Diane, who is probably the single greatest influence on me. Her love, support, and patience are invaluable to me.

A woman in my life named Linda Griebel is known as my administrative assistant. Actually, it would be more accurate to call her "the glue that holds my professional life together." Her integrity as a work partner makes life so much easier, and she has my heartfelt thanks.

I'd like to thank my agent, John Ware, for his support and unwavering willingness to sail on despite some stormy literary seas. I appreciate his commitment and drive.

I want to gratefully acknowledge my editor, Charles Gerras, who should probably be considered a co-author given all the time, energy, and expertise he put into this project! His extraordinary efforts are greatly appreciated.

Finally, I'd like to thank my family and friends who are all eternally positive and supportive of my efforts. They provide a wonderful framework for helping me live my life.

Introduction

Among the many social vestiges of the 1960s—Woodstock, hippies, yippies, Elvis, the Beatles, burning bras and draft cards, two Kennedy assassinations—is a generation of people who grew up defiantly questioning established ways and resisting the pressure to conform. The radical changes of those volatile years still linger in the national psyche. And the echoes take that same generation down a path of quiet suffering unprecedented in America and, probably, in the world.

Of course, many positive changes also took place during those years and after—advances in civil rights, greater mobility and freedom of choice, a more individual and (theoretically, anyway) personally satisfying lifestyle, and less time spent in physical drudgery. But all these gains did not come without cost. Getting high, once taken lightly as an exploration of consciousness, has ushered in a nightmare drug problem. AIDS has made "free love" something that could cost you your life. Relationships that endure "till death do us part" are largely confined to couples over 60 and classic late-night movies.

Add to these obvious costs the deterioration of our national mental health. A startling new finding shows that the incidence of depression has increased nearly tenfold among those born since World War II—the so-called Baby Boomers. Like all the other Boomers, I was raised in a social environment unlike any that previously existed. The 1950s, 1960s, and 1970s were turbulent times that forever changed the face of American values and lifestyles—and, apparently, the internal feelings Americans have about themselves and their world.

The astonishing increase in clinical depression is highly significant. It means faulty biology probably isn't the chief cause of this problem, because we know that human genetics and biochemistry do not change so dramatically over a single generation.

Social change, however, *is* swift and dramatic. The factors that have significantly raised the level of depression are clearly far more likely to be environmental than biological. Thus, one hope for depressed people of all ages lies in understanding which psychological and cultural factors brought on these high rates of depression so quickly. Then we can learn to handle them.

Depression affects people of *all* ages, but the strong concentration of depression among the Boomers is a sort of window that helps highlight the underlying factors of this serious problem. That allows us to devise realistic ways of addressing depression effectively.

This book starts with deliberate and practical guidelines that help you understand where your depression comes from, and it follows up with effective ways to overcome it. I believe that solutions to your problems become more readily apparent and more easily applied once you learn what you are dealing with. Then I can teach you about many effective measures for overcoming the problems associated with feeling bad.

How Did You Get into This Mess?

You will learn about factors that lead to depression. Then I will explore the possible causes and associated symptoms, such as anxiety, pessimism, an overwhelming sense of helplessness and hopelessness, troubled relationships, and poor self-esteem. You will discover how these factors can be identified in you. Best of all, you will see how they can be handled, and your depression overcome.

It's good news for you that depression is more responsive to treatment than almost any other psychological problem. When the treatment is aimed in the right direction, then organized and carried out appropriately, symptoms of depression typically disappear in a hurry. I will show you how to play a positive role in this process.

As one who regularly treats depressed people, I have been deeply moved by the despair and pain I see. This concern led me to develop a deeper understanding of this problem and what to do about it. I felt an urgency to develop more rapid and effective treatments, knowing that every day spent impaired by depression is costly to you on many levels. The result is a highly effective way of thinking about and treating depression. My methods were once available only to my professional colleagues; now I present them to you. Self-help is not only possible for those who suffer from depression, it is *necessary* for a full and lasting recovery.

The inescapable conclusion is that our lifestyles and values, both cultural and personal, affect our sense of well-being. In these pages, I identify many of the key lifestyle patterns, including ways you think and ways you relate to others, that can either encourage or prevent depression.

You will learn to recognize any destructive patterns that might exist in the way you do things. Once you know which patterns lead you to disappointment or despair, you are in a position to make positive changes. Then you can teach yourself new ways of doing things to improve your life. Your primary goal is to *feel good* about who you are and what you do.

I believe that depression is generally a product of an imbalance in some lifestyle arena, some important element omitted from your experience. Relief comes from reestablishing that balance through new and useful experiences. This book helps you to do that through structured learning experiences. It means you learn by *doing,* not just by spinning "Don't Worry, Be Happy" thoughts around in your head.

Suppose I tell you to cheer up. Why isn't that enough to help you? It tells you what to do. Not only that, it tells you what you *must* do to feel better. Why doesn't it provide relief? Clearly, knowing what to do does not translate into having the skills to do it. So this book focuses heavily on *how* to do the things you must do to fight depression successfully.

Throughout this book, you will find many examples involving good, intelligent, healthy people who sink into depression when their lives don't match their desires. Sometimes they know why they are depressed but don't know what to do about it; other times, they have absolutely no idea why life seems so painful.

Developing life skills and resources to draw on when facing life's difficult demands is the key to living depression-free. And that's the thrust of this book. If you are depressed, you must learn to identify the lifestyle patterns that lead to depression and how they apply to you. I know you will enjoy developing these skills. They will help you manage your life better and get more of what you want out of it.

If other people are doing the things you want to do, obviously they're doable. Your job is to learn *how* they're done so you can do them, too. It is my job to explain those how-to's in a way that makes sense to you.

Plan to be an active force in your own recovery from depression by participating in the exercises and answering the thought-provoking questions scattered throughout the book. As your thinking and responses change, relief from depression will follow. Once you learn how to respond to situations by using a greater variety of skills and clearer thinking, you are in a stronger position to prevent future episodes of depression.

How You Can Make the Most of This Book

The methods I use in this book do not rehash the past. I believe you're reading this book with the hope that things will be better in the future—next week, next month, next year, and all the rest of the years of your life. Thus, the focus is on change with an eye to the future. With that in mind, I provide new ways of looking at depression, plus opportunities for learning by experience, because ultimately, that's how we learn best. It is the things that happen in your everyday life—your interactions with others and your private activities—that shape your perceptions and attitudes and govern the course of your actions.

In that regard, I must emphasize that the best way to benefit from this book is to *participate* in the activities I suggest in each chapter. *Doing* is the operative word here.

You have a great deal to look forward to in the pages that follow. I know you will benefit in ways that will lead you to the contentment and success you desire.

Chapter 1

GET TO KNOW THE FACE
OF DEPRESSION

Donna sat in front of me, sobbing and trying to catch her breath as she repeatedly pressed a tissue to her face to wipe away her tears. It was not unusual for Donna to cry during our therapy sessions. It usually began soon after she arrived, no matter what my opening remark was.

From our very first session, it was obvious that Donna was in a lot of emotional pain. She had seen other therapists on and off throughout her 40 years, but none of them had been able to help. An intelligent, articulate, and attractive woman, Donna saw herself as a total failure. She had battled drugs and alcohol abuse most of her life. Married and divorced three times, she was struggling to raise her four children alone. Donna was highly dependent on others and became very anxious if left on her own for very long. She barely managed in her job because she was so prone to emotional outbursts.

Donna was obsessed with her desire to have a man around, to be there for her in every way, to rescue her from the unpleasant realities of her life. As a result, she got involved with some pretty strange men whom she should have avoided. Naturally, these destructive episodes made her feel even worse about herself, increasing her depression and further impairing her ability to function.

Donna describes her most recent sufferings to me, and then she pauses and waits for me to say or do something to alleviate her pain and get her life moving in a positive direction. But because I know that Donna has been fighting just to survive since she fled her abusive home at age 15, I also know that clichés about dark clouds with silver linings and better tomorrows won't help.

The things Donna wants are reasonable and positive—a healthy and committed relationship with a man, better coping skills to ease her need to escape through drinks and drugs, more positive experiences, and a steadier approach to life. However, Donna's way of going after these things actually prevents her from achieving them.

SMALL TURNING POINTS
CAN BRING BIG CHANGES

I find that a person's life usually has many small turning points rather than a single huge one. So in one of my sessions with Donna, I deliberately mentioned my plan to go hiking in the mountains with one of my female friends later that week. I had often told Donna about my love of the outdoors and its role as a necessary counterbalance to the stresses of my life. Such steadying influences in life are vital to maintaining a sense of well-being. I hoped Donna would eventually come to master that skill. Currently she had virtually no recreation in her life. She did nothing but work.

Donna seemed mildly interested in my hiking plans, though she admitted she had never gone on a hike in her life. I surprised her with an invitation to join my friend and me. She was immediately gripped by mixed feelings. She wanted to go, yet was afraid to go. Donna asked for and received plenty of reassurance that this beautiful hike would not exceed her physical abilities.

Days later, as we approached the state park where we would hike, I pointed out Stonewall Peak, our destination. Donna looked panicked, then helpless, as she viewed the impressive peak. "I don't think I can do it," she said quietly. She had an image of our laboring intensely as we climbed straight up the vertical side of the mountain, our lives in constant danger. She had no experience, no way to know that our climb would be safe and easy due to a continuous series of switchbacks (small inclines that reverse on themselves) gradually leading to the top.

Hesitantly, proceeding on trust alone, Donna began the hike with us. Once on the trail, after a few switchbacks, Donna began to relax and enjoy the beauty and peacefulness of the place. Soon she was laughing about her original fears, and all along the trail she was more alive and happy than I'd ever seen her.

A few rest stops and several snacks later, we were at the top looking down on the rest of the world. Donna was delighted, wonderfully animated, and pleased with herself.

All the way back she talked about other hikes she'd heard of and would like to try. A whole new world opened up for Donna in that one morning. It didn't matter if she ever hiked again; the important thing was the valuable lesson she learned from the experience. Donna saw the peak, the goal, and she automatically saw it as too overwhelming for her to achieve because she didn't know how to get there. Donna was ready to give up before she even tried! Yet, with a realistic and appropriate strategy, she reached the goal and experienced the proud satisfaction of having done so.

That hike was a turning point in Donna's thinking. She had seen for herself that she could succeed in conquering a daunting challenge, just as others do all the time. Up to then, instead of learning how to reach her goal, Donna had focused only on her supposed shortcomings. This hike led her to think in terms of learning to develop a realistic plan to achieve her desires. She learned that most goals lie at the end of *at least* one specific path, and she learned to separate achievable goals from impossible ones.

Now Donna knows she's as competent as anyone, once she learns how to do something properly. Not knowing how to do something merely reflects a lack of experience, nothing more—not inadequacy and not a lack of intelligence.

WHERE DOES DEPRESSION COME FROM?

To understand Donna's depression, and your own, too, it's important to see that the things she wanted most were missing from her life. She valued relationships highly and had none to speak of. She wanted to have fun in her life, but she focused only on life's problems, not the solutions. She felt trapped in a negative world, powerless to change. So Donna stayed depressed.

People who develop ineffective ways to manage life's demands get hurt when they fail at anything they don't know how to do well. No matter what the aim is—a loving relationship, a job promotion, an attractive appearance, strong self-esteem—depression is a predictable result of feeling powerless to experience what matters to you. I frequently see clients in therapy who hurt terribly because they can't get the approval, the recognition, the love, the support, the intimacy, or the self-acceptance they want, along with any of the other psychological necessities for a happy life.

HOW THERAPISTS DEAL WITH DEPRESSION

About 30 to 40 million Americans suffer from depression in varying degrees, so it's no wonder that the mental health profession gives this problem so much attention. As a result, several intelligent theories and effective treatments have been developed over the years.

■ The *biological approach* assumes that depression is caused by a chemical imbalance in the brain. Treatment usually involves antidepressant medications.

■ The *interpersonal approach* sees depression as a consequence of hurtful and ineffective relationships. Teaching healthy and positive relationship skills is the treatment of choice.

■ A third general approach involves adjusting a person's *cognitive (thinking) style*.

One cognitive approach, developed by Aaron Beck, M.D., emphasizes errors in thinking that are not apparent to the sufferer but are obvious to the trained therapist. Treatment involves identifying distorted thoughts and correcting them in therapy.

A second cognitive approach focuses on *attributional style*, the way we explain to ourselves the things that happen in our lives. Depressed individuals generally explain life events in a way that perpetuates their depression.

Since I will focus on *your* attributional style throughout this book, I want to explain it clearly. As an example, suppose you were denied a raise you asked for and felt you deserved.

■ Would you attribute it to a personal (*internal*) shortcoming ("I'm not good enough") or to a situational (*external*) cause ("The company is having financial difficulties")?

■ Would it be a general (*global*) interpretation ("I'm worthless") or a specific one ("I'm not performing this job as well as I could")?

■ Would it be an unchanging (*stable*) explanation ("It will *always* be this way") or a changing (*unstable*) one ("I'll get my raise when company finances improve")?

Those with attributional errors are taught to make their attributions more realistic. In other words, the depressed person learns to become more objective in explaining the relationship between cause and effect.

A third cognitive approach, called *learned helplessness,* was developed by Martin Seligman, Ph.D. This approach views a person's depression as a result of his being subjected to hurtful situations that are inescapable. For example, if you grow up in a family where you are subjected to violence or arbitrary punishments, you may conclude, when abused by others, that nothing can be done. Later, the situation may change to one in which you *can* do something to escape hurts, but because of previous conditioning you do nothing to help yourself. This is learned helplessness. You withdraw, give up, and retreat into a state of depression, painfully accepting what seems to be an unchangeable situation.

The cure for learned helplessness lies in discovering that you really have more control over life events than you think. You must learn how to recognize and use that control. Unrealistic perceptions about control play a major role in the experience of depression, a phenomenon I will explore in a later chapter.

CHOICES AND LIFESTYLE
CAN TRIGGER DEPRESSION

Each theory I described above focuses on one particular aspect of depression—cognitive, social, or physical. I propose a unique and broader view. I say depression encompasses *all* these aspects—and more. The way you think, the way you interact with others, the way you relate to your body—all these are shaped by your background and experience, and you develop set patterns as a result. You will get much further in your self-help efforts if you realize how a single personality pattern influences many of your lifestyle choices. For example, if you find it hard to say no, you probably avoid confrontations whenever possible, you get anxious in the presence of aggression, and you work hard to keep peace; you are easily intimidated by others and show similar reactions in countless other situations. If you can't say no, your self-image suffers, your view of others becomes cynical, and the repeated manipulation you suffer under others confirms your negative impressions. You think you can't change the pattern, so you become its victim. Victims of *any* sort are at high risk for depression.

My treatment for depression emphasizes learning to identify and change the patterns that cause that mental state. I provide many methods that help break hurtful patterns and build useful ones.

As you can see, there is no single cause for depression. If you could be an invisible presence when I talk to my depressed clients, you'd know how varied the symptoms are and how many kinds of life situations can lead to depression. You would find out how these intelligent, sensitive people made depression a lifestyle by trying to achieve goals with methods that not only *did not work* but *could not work*. Their repeated mistakes in coping with these failures and hurts make them see life as a painful passage, something to endure rather than enjoy.

Perhaps depression is best viewed as a lifestyle that is based on repetitive but unrewarding patterns of thinking, feeling, and behaving that you somehow manage to live with. But these patterns actually interfere with achieving your life's goals. Depression is a predictable consequence of an imbalance in your lifestyle that robs you of the things you value most.

If you are depressed, you probably have a genuine desire to change, just so you can experience some relief. But you've probably had insensitive people suggest that "if you *really* wanted to change, you would." So you know I'm right when I state that the desire to change is simply not enough.

No matter how motivated you are, facing east to watch a sunset won't get you the view you want. You have to find a realistic way to accomplish your aims. I assume that if you knew how to change and feel better, you would have done it by now. Perhaps you, like my clients, simply do not know how to help yourself; like them, you only know you feel terrible. That's where I come in. I help people identify the patterns that cause them hurt and help them build new experiences and strengthen abilities that will let them experience happiness and success.

WHAT CURES DEPRESSION?

Throughout this book, I encourage you to examine your attitude toward everyday living, based on what your previous experiences have taught you. Such self-awareness is necessary if you are to discover which skills would be the most useful for you to develop in your efforts to defeat depression.

If you suffer from depression now, or if you feel vulnerable to future episodes of depression, it is essential to appreciate this point: If what you're doing in your life isn't bringing about the things you want from life or preventing the episodes of depression that led you to buy this book, clearly *you need to do something else*. This is a theme I will return to often.

Unfortunately, it is my experience that most people who are depressed don't realize they can try something else. They certainly do not know what that alternative action might be. And that's exactly why they continue to repeat the same mistakes, which result in the same pain and failure.

I want to acquaint you with a new perspective on dealing with depression that has brought highly successful results. I also want to share the good news that *you can do a great deal to help yourself quickly and effectively*. Depression will lift when you balance inner comfort and outer competence in your life.

DOES YOUR DEPRESSION *NEED* TREATMENT?

Sometimes depression is a normal reaction to hurtful or stressful circumstances, like a divorce, the death of a loved one, or the loss of a job. In such a case, I become concerned as a clinician only if your depression persists beyond a reasonable period, or if it is so severe that it interferes with your ability to function effectively. When the depression is so pervasive that it takes over your life, far beyond a reaction to a particular stressful event, it needs to be addressed as a problem.

It is very important for you to know that no one is happy or satisfied *all* the time. I am sure you have seen celebrity interviews where big stars with plenty of money, vast numbers of admiring and loyal fans, and seemingly unlimited opportunities confess to being unhappy. They say it's because of things they don't have, or because of their inability to enjoy the things they do have.

The fact that the incidence of depression has increased so much so fast suggests that environmental factors play a greater role in depression than body chemistry or genetics. Until the last few years, little was known about the roots of depression or possible cures for it. The advice a depressed client received from a therapist was likely to be identical to that received from friends: "Cheer up! Look at the bright side of life." Superficial as it sounds, such advice is technically correct. A depressed person who comes for treatment *wants* to cheer up! What's missing is a plan for how to do it.

▶ LOOK DEEPER
Take Stock of Your Emotional Discomfort

Only you truly know what degree of emotional discomfort you are experiencing. No checklist an observer provides could accurately reflect your day-to-day struggle. So, rather than try to adapt yourself to some type of depression-state inventory, you can better assess your needs by simply responding to these questions.

- Am I satisfied with the quality of my life?
- Does life hold positive meaning and purpose for me?
- Do I feel good about myself most of the time?
- Am I living life as I want to live it?
- Am I successful in achieving the things that matter to me?
- Do I have a sense of balance that allows for a richness and diversity of experiences on many levels?

Take the time to review each of these questions deliberately. Consider your answers carefully. It's essential that you be honest with yourself, so you know just where to start getting your life in order.

APPROACH THE PROBLEM INTELLIGENTLY

My purpose is to teach you about ideas and techniques that will help you make better choices in the way you respond to life's demands. Just remember that thinking about something is *not* the same as doing it. Donna's story proved that point. Her thoughts about hiking could never have been as vivid and powerful as her *experience* as a hiker. Her positive insights were the direct result of *doing something different.* I urge you to test the ideas and do the exercises I present as a way to create new experiences that will help you. These new experiences will show you the importance of personal growth, mental balance, and the ability to adapt to unexpected or unwanted change.

As you read, keep your individual needs and your individual approach to life in mind. This is not a book about depressed people, it's about *you* and what *you* can do to feel better.

LOOK DEEPER

Make the Most of This Opportunity

How do you feel right now? Hopeless? Hopeful? Intrigued? Overwhelmed? How does that feeling color your expectations of benefit from this book? Take a positive approach and learn what you can to improve your response to life. Chances are that you'll be happily surprised with the result.

KEY POINTS TO REMEMBER

- Depression reflects an imbalance in key areas of your life.
- The things that you want are probably realistic and worthwhile. Your problem is a lack of skill in obtaining these things.
- If you're missing out on experiences you desire, it isn't because you're unable to have them. It's because you haven't learned how.
- Incompetence usually reflects a lack of experience, not a lack of ability.
- Depression affects 30 to 40 million people in the United States.
- Theories about depression abound, and treatments cover a wide range, from biological to psychological.
- The biological approach assumes depression is due to an imbalance of brain chemistry.
- The interpersonal approach blames depression on hurtful relationships.
- The cognitive approach sees depression as a product of errors in thinking.
- Attributional style refers to the way you explain life events to yourself.
- In all treatments for depression, clear thinking is emphasized as a goal.
- The lifestyle treatment for depression emphasizes learning to identify and change the patterns in your life that made you depressed.
- There is no one single cause for depression.
- The *desire* to change is simply not enough; you need realistic methods for doing so.
- Depression will lift when you attain balance between inner comfort and external competence.

Chapter 2

DISCOVER THE MANY MASKS DEPRESSION CAN WEAR

There is a popular bumper sticker that says, "Life is a bitch, and then you die." People who are not depressed find the bumper sticker amusing. Those in the throes of depression tend to nod their heads in solemn agreement.

The hassles of life simply overwhelm the ability of some people to cope realistically. Others somehow navigate the complications of life, but the effort exhausts them. Since stress is a basic component of depression, and we all experience and manage stress in our own way, it's easy to see why depression takes so many different forms and presents such a diagnostic challenge. This is one reason why many people who are depressed don't even know it.

DIAGNOSING ALEX'S AIMLESSNESS

Alex came to therapy hoping for a way to overcome what he called his aimlessness. In his late thirties, Alex had been unemployed for about a month. His most recent job as a program planner and administrator came to an abrupt end when funding for his program was cut off.

Alex, married for 16 years, described his wife as "ambitious for me." Her attempts to motivate him to get a new job led to constant friction between them. Alex said they caused him to feel emotionally abandoned. He realized he needed to work again soon, since the financial burden was too great to manage solely on his wife's income, but he couldn't seem to face job-hunting.

Alex blamed his constant anxiety on his employment worries. He could not decide whether to work for someone else or begin his own business. He said his tendency to be a perfectionist was one reason that he did not want to make any job decisions unless he was absolutely sure they were the correct ones. Naturally, he could not pursue interviews for jobs until a clear goal—start a business or work for someone—had been established. But how could he make plans to start his own business until he *knew* he could pull it off?

Alex complained that his attention span had become short, that he could no longer follow through on business ideas or even mundane domestic tasks. His wife was frustrated with him. His friends annoyed him by asking about his job plans. He saw no potential for help from his family, since "they are a part of my original self-esteem problem." Alex was sleeping poorly, awakening early much of the time, and he could find little that was good in his life. So Alex turned to therapy for some answers.

The original complaint was aimlessness, but Alex was also experiencing poor motivation, anxiety, indecisiveness, paralyzing perfectionism, diminished concentration, social isolation, marital discord, poor self-esteem, sleep disturbance, fatigue, and a lost sense of pleasure. With all these warning signs, even an amateur could have said, "Gee, I think you're depressed." And yet Alex never realized it! It may seem odd to you that a person could have so many symptoms of depression and still not recognize it, but I can tell you, it happens all the time.

THE EXPERIENCE OF DEPRESSION

If you feel down, feel blue, are miserable with your life, feel trapped, have a negative attitude, or see things darkly, you're experiencing a form of depression. Its presence makes life seem too much to cope with and not at all that worthwhile anyway.

Depression is truly a universal experience; *everyone* goes through it at one time or another, to a greater or lesser degree. The line separating *normal* depression from *clinical* depression has not yet been clearly drawn. That is why I suggested earlier that only you know the depth of the discomfort you are experiencing.

Now let's consider the many different ways depression surfaces. Being familiar with all of its manifestations will enhance your self-awareness. Then you can apply the self-help strategies in this book more effectively.

I know you want immediate solutions, but focusing on quick-fix answers is usually part of the depression problem. It leads people to try formula answers that aren't really appropriate. So use this chapter to help gauge the extent of *your* depression. Then later chapters will teach you what to do about it. Keep in mind that *your* experience of depression will be unique in some ways, but also similar in some ways to that of others.

Because depression's causes and symptoms may vary so much from individual to individual, you need some guidelines so you can recognize what's going on in your own case. The numerous examples and information that follow will help you figure out where to concentrate your efforts. For example, if your relationships are the problem, but you focus only on your own distorted thoughts and miss opportunities to improve your interactions, you're squandering lifesaving opportunities by misdirection.

Remember Alex? If I had concentrated on treating only the aimlessness he complained about, I might have missed all the other things that were hurting him. You can't always settle for the convenient answer. It's like the old joke about the not-so-bright fellow looking for his lost wallet under a street light. Asked by a passerby if that was where he last had it in his possession, he answered, "No, but the light to search by is better here."

The point, of course, is that you can do a very fine job of helping yourself defeat depression with techniques you will learn later, but first you'll need to know which patterns in which areas

TAKE ACTION

What Makes You Think You're Depressed?

How do you know you are depressed? What symptoms or patterns do you see in yourself that make you think you are depressed? List them *before* you read on. Later you'll learn about other symptoms of depression you can add to your list if they apply to you. Don't stop at ten if you have more symptoms.

1 _____

2 _____

3 _____

4 _____

5 _____

6 _____

7 _____

8 _____

9 _____

10 _____

or dimensions of your life are at the seat of the problem. There are no set formulas for help, only individual approaches.

ASPECTS OF DEPRESSION'S SYMPTOMS

I find it useful to see patterns in the symptoms of my depressed clients according to different aspects of their experience—physical symptoms, behavioral problems, distorted thinking, mood and emotional difficulties, troubled relationships, specific situations that trigger episodes of depression, spiritual or symbolic meaning attached to depression, and the personal history that generated lifestyle patterns related to depression.

It is important to learn how you experience depression, so you can address the most relevant issues associated with it. Otherwise, you may focus on irrelevant issues and delay improvement. For example, if your depression usually surfaces in specific situations, such as when you go to parties or go home to visit your parents, then taking drugs (even prescribed medications) that operate on a physical basis is not a very logical solution.

Let's consider each potential area of depression and its related symptoms separately, so you can better understand the way you experience depression. I start with a case that illustrates the key points of each aspect.

Bill's Body Announces Depression
The Physical Dimension

Bill woke up with a start. True to his pattern, he strained to hear any unusual sounds that might have caused him to awaken. "All I hear is the sound of Cindy breathing deeply as she sleeps next to me," he thought. "Dammit, I'd give anything to be like her and be asleep right now."

Satisfied that nothing unusual had wakened him, Bill looked

at the clock and realized that he didn't need to get up for another two hours. His mind raced and spun as ideas about his work and events left hanging from yesterday collided with plans for things he would need to do that day. "Why am I spinning all this stuff around in my head when I should be asleep? Another day of the same damn thing—wake up so early, lie in bed trying to fall back to sleep, flash on everything I hate about my life, feel tired as hell all day from not sleeping, go to bed thinking I'm so tired I'll sleep great, and then start the same damn cycle all over again tomorrow. Who am I kidding? There is something wrong with me—maybe I should see a sleep specialist or something."

Bill turned away from the clock that kept telling him, in hours and minutes, how much sleep he *wasn't* getting. Thinking he had a sleep disorder, and that a sleep specialist might somehow help him, made Bill feel a little better for the moment. "I'll probably just need some kind of sleeping pill for a little while until I learn to relax more," he decided. When he finally got out of bed after a half hour of tossing and turning, Bill looked at Cindy and wished she were awake, too. A pang of guilt for thinking that passed through him and lingered a while as he watched her sleep. He tried to remember the last time they had made love, but he couldn't. It had been quite a while since he'd felt any desire to.

With his mind still racing along, filled with concerns that ultimately proved unimportant, Bill turned on the television and watched a program on gardening. Nothing else was on. "I hate this. I wish I could sleep and wake up feeling rested and refreshed just once. Instead I'm sitting here alone, watching this junk while Cindy and the rest of the world snooze on with not a care in the world."

By the time Cindy got up, Bill could barely contain his irritation at the fact that she'd slept so well and wakened so cheerful. "God, I hate mornings," Bill said out loud to no one in particular as he shaved. "They are the worst part of my day. And today is going to be rotten—I can tell already. But then, most days are." Bill pushed himself through the morning routine of shaving, showering, dressing, and mumbling a few words to Cindy, and then he headed to work.

He was tired already and dreaded the prospect of a full day at his desk on so little sleep. His anxiety level rose as he thought of all the things he planned to do at work. Bill put on his socially acceptable (but totally phony) smile for the day as he entered the office and proceeded to carry out his day's tasks. On his way home that evening, Bill realized he'd forgotten to follow up on his plan to see a sleep specialist. "Maybe I just have an unusual metabolism and must learn to accept it," he said to himself most unconvincingly. Then his thoughts turned to the evening news and what Cindy would cook for dinner, even though he didn't feel like eating. Too early (again) the next morning, Bill sat learning new techniques for growing his own tomatoes.

Dissecting Bill's Blues

Bill shows some of the classic physical signs of depression: early-morning wakening (one form of insomnia commonly experienced by depressed people), rumination of thoughts, fatigue and lethargy, feeling worse in the morning, anxiety, a diminished sex drive, and a decreased appetite.

Most of Bill's symptoms are of a physical nature, but beyond what Bill shows, there are other common physical symptoms of depression as well. These include excessive sleeping (unlike Bill's insomnia), excessive appetite (unlike Bill's diminished appetite), a marked change in body weight associated with the change in appetite, vague physical complaints with no detectable cause, or exaggerated physical complaints whose cause is clear.

The physical symptoms of depression often lead a person to seek help from a physician. (The family doctor, or the general practitioner, is the first one most likely to encounter depressed individuals.) It takes a knowledgeable and experienced doctor to identify symptoms of depression and make appropriate recommendations because *many depressive symptoms can be associated*

↳ **LOOK DEEPER**

Medication or Action for Depression?

The evidence indicates that most depression is *not* physically based. Then how is it that a lifestyle problem like depression can have such clearly physical symptoms? Is it reasonable to treat such symptoms physically, as with medication? Can such treatment distract from the real problem?

---

with literally dozens of different physical problems. So, if you suspect that you suffer from depression, start with a thorough physical examination and have a frank talk with your doctor about your symptoms and concerns.

Danny Turns Nasty
The Behavioral Dimension

On his way home from work, Danny stopped to buy Vicki some flowers. He felt bad about the fight they'd had before he left for work that morning. He struggled to remember what started the fight, but as usual, he couldn't. He had been a bit grumpier than usual, but Vicki knew Danny was never Mr. Sunshine in the morning. She had learned to keep what little conversation he tolerated neutral. Mostly, she just gave him lots of quiet company.

Suddenly Danny remembered the remark that had set him off. Vicki had mentioned, all too damn casually for his taste, that she'd be stopping at her friend Judy's house after work to see the new furniture. "Women!" he had raged to himself. "There are a million things that need to be done around here, and she's off to see furniture. She's never around when I need something, but just let one of her friends call her for something stupid like new decor and she's right there."

Thinking about this now puzzled him. "Is that really the way I felt this morning? Is that why I blew up?" Danny didn't remember thinking *anything* this morning when Vicki announced her intentions. He was only aware of rage. He didn't even realize he was screaming at her until she ran into the bedroom and locked the door. He decided he didn't have time for her hide-and-seek games, so he left for work, slamming the door on his way out.

As he drove to work, weaving in and out of traffic, Danny made plenty of obscene, angry gestures to all the rotten drivers he encountered. His sadness caught up to him while he was stopped at a light, and he shuddered and began to cry. He tried to control it, but this crying episode was like most of the others; it seemed to come upon him suddenly and from out of nowhere. "Too bad it never leaves as suddenly as it comes," he mused.

Danny stopped for a quick breakfast, and when it wasn't quick enough, he demanded to see the manager. The manager was just a kid, barely older than the one who took his order. Danny was hoping for a more formidable opponent. He yelled his piece anyway, finally got his food, and wolfed it down. No one was unhappy to see him leave.

When Danny got to work, things went from bad to worse—incompetent employees and supervisors, stupid policies, ridiculous procedures, all glowing in neon that only Danny is perceptive enough to see. Never strong on giving compliments anyway, Danny couldn't think of a single positive thing to say to anybody on this day (though he thought he should try to). When nothing came to mind, he closed his office door and reached way back in his desk drawer for the bottle. "Relief is on the way!" He really didn't feel right about this source of relief, but he thought he owed it to everyone else to try to mellow a little. That is when he thought about picking up some flowers for Vicki on the way home. He cried one other time that day, and only for a little while. He was gentle as a lamb after that.

What Lights Danny's Fuse?

Danny is not the guy you want to spend your summer vacation with. Yet, when he's not raging around, he is truly a nice person. What is this Dr. Jekyll/Mr. Hyde thing that happens with Danny?

Danny's explosiveness indicates how easily he is upset, how quickly he gets frustrated (called low frustration tolerance), and how out of control his behavior can get when his feelings seem too strong to contain. He tries to manage his angry feelings, but as long as he feels misunderstood and sees himself as a victim of everyone else's incompetence (or insensitivity), he will likely go on getting angrier and angrier. Only someone who is a martyr (or is foolish enough to put up with such behavior) will stay with Danny. And of course, if Vicki leaves him for her own sake, Danny will feel even more a victim of the insensitivity of others and probably will get even angrier and more depressed. In this way, Danny illustrated well the self-defeating repetitive patterns of depression, highlighting the need to recognize and manage both our feelings and our life circumstances.

Danny's use of alcohol to "medicate" himself is a typical but unfortunate choice. Alcohol is a depressant; for someone who is already depressed, it is simply a bad drug, to be avoided.

Many of Danny's behavior patterns are common in depressed individuals: temper displays, aggressive behavior, acting out feelings in ways that are impulsive, even at odds with true feelings,

LOOK DEEPER

Examine the Feelings/Behavior Link

How would you describe the relationship between behavior and feelings? Does your behavior consistently reflect your feelings? Explain why or why not.

perfectionistic behavior, substance abuse, and crying spells. Other behaviors common to depression include marked changes in a person's activity level (usually a decrease), suicide attempts, slowed movement and slurred speech, agitated and anxious behaviors (such as pacing), and resignation (no longer trying to change things for the better). Keep in mind, *no single behavior is an indicator of depression,* but it may be a signal of trouble spots.

How a Phone Call Paralyzed Linda
The Situational (Contextual) Dimension

The telephone rang several times before the sound penetrated Linda's deep sleep. She silently cursed whoever had wakened her so early on a Sunday morning. The inimitable voice that barked "Hello" on the other end could only have been her father's. Who else could be such a royal pain even from a thousand miles away? When he asked with feigned innocence, "Oh, did I wake you?" Linda wanted to give a sarcastic reply, but instead she meekly answered, "No, I was just getting up." Not that he would have cared if she had told him the truth. When a father calls his daughter, no matter the time, she should be thrilled to hear from him. Genuinely thrilled. Linda learned years ago that it was best to meet his expectations. She asked how he was.

Dad ignored her polite inquiry and announced his intention to come for a visit. Linda's heart sank, but she tried to sound happily surprised. "How come, Dad? You were just here a couple of months ago." When he replied that he could use the rest, Linda silently responded, "So could I." Then she felt guilty. She wondered whether other young women felt as she did about their fathers, or whether she was some really terrible person who just couldn't deal with being around her dad. Was she immature, or somehow emotionally screwed up?

But Linda really didn't see herself that way. She was a successful and competent woman. She lived alone and did it well. She managed her dating relationships effectively, staying out of risky situations and avoiding men who were bad news. She supported herself on a decent, if not generous, salary, had good friends, and was in excellent physical shape due to a regimen of good diet and dance classes. Her job, running an office for four busy professionals, was going well and gave her plenty of gratification.

Why was she able to handle every part of her life so well, yet mess up in her relationship with her dad? Somehow he made her feel so small, so insignificant, that she just hated being around him. His fierce temper precluded raising any subject he didn't like, and he sure didn't like talking about his relationship with Linda. Daughters do what fathers say. Period. End of discussion.

Linda hung up after mumbling some affectionate words she didn't really mean. And the world went ugly. Counting the two weeks before he came, then the week of his visit, and at least a week of recovery after, she saw a full month of depression stretching out before her. How she hated feeling so weak around her father. Fantasies of telling him off, even using physical violence against him, floated through her mind. Sometimes she enjoyed the fantasies and even felt better for having had them, but then she felt worse when she admitted to herself she was too much of a wimp to do anything but cater to his every whim. As she recalled every spanking, every shouting match, every embarrassment, she decided to stay in bed for the day, feeling too depressed to go anywhere or do anything.

When Monday came, it took all the energy she could muster to call in sick. Her father would certainly have disapproved of her irresponsible decision, and she berated herself for it in his absence. Linda spent the rest of the day deciding whether to be on time or make him wait at the airport when he arrived. She finally decided to decide later.

Linda's Lucky: Cause and Cure Are Clear

For many people, episodes of depression have specific triggers—people, places, objects, and times (like the holidays or anniversaries, even certain times of the day, week, or month).

TAKE ACTION

Foster Positive Feelings about Yourself

Keep a sharp eye on TV news stories that center on ordinary citizens, and note the role circumstance plays in their behavior, feelings, and thoughts. If you were in these situations, think of ways you could create positive responses in yourself.

See the examples to help you identify situations that amplify your strong points.

Situation	Skills Amplified
Take a class.	Ability to learn easily Ability to relate to others
Take a hiking trip.	Powers of self-reliance Knowledge of camping techniques Ability to endure hardships
Write a family history.	Talent for writing Ability to do research Knack for reporting Gift for organization

---

In situational depression, the person manages well until overwhelmed by a particular context. Linda, for example, does a good job of managing her life until she has to deal with her father. Then, for whatever reason, and you can guess dozens, Linda becomes helpless and passive. Nowhere else in her life does this occur. She is depressed for extended periods whenever her father enters her life, however brief the time.

Whenever depression is so clearly related to a situation, the chances for recovery are great. The straightforward solution lies in learning to manage the troublesome situation in a way that will prevent the victim mind-set that can lead to depression. You can create emotional distance from the anniversary of a loved one's death, the date of a breakup, or any other painful experience. New learning and experiences can skillfully be created to disconnect old triggers.

One type of depression, seasonal affective disorder (SAD), is worthy of your special attention. Sufferers lapse into depression with winter's shorter days and don't recover until spring. Considerable evidence suggests that SAD is biologically based in susceptible people who must have a certain quota of daylight-stimulated brain chemicals. The cure is amazingly simple: extra hours spent each day carrying out normal activities while exposed to a special type of fluorescent light. Consult a physician if you think this may be your problem.

Wendy Wakes Up from a Nightmare
The Symbolic Dimension

Wendy was unusually slow to wake up. For reasons unknown, it took forever to open and focus her eyes and too long to get her mind to work. She was scared, but why? Wendy was startled to see she was not in her bed. For a frightening, extended moment, she didn't know where she was. Then a page for Dr. Harris that boomed over the public address system helped her realize that she was in a hospital bed. A nurse appeared and immediately provided the orientation Wendy needed. "You are in University Hospital. You were attacked and beaten. You have lots of cuts, bruises, and swelling, but nothing is broken and you will undoubtedly recover completely. You'll be here for a couple of days until you're strong enough to go home and we're sure you're okay."

Wendy was relieved to know where she was and that she would recover completely. Then, like a punch in the stomach, Wendy was bombarded with frightening and overwhelming images. She tried to move and cried out from the pain. She lay still and felt unreal while the fragmented memories surged into her awareness: pulling into a tight space in the parking garage near the gym. Looking forward to a good workout. Grabbing her gym bag, locking the car. A crazed man, screaming, a tormented expression on his face, grabbing her, knocking her down, beating her . . . waking up here.

Wendy shuddered involuntarily. She tried to remember more of what happened, but she couldn't. It was all too quick for her mind to record the incident.

And then came the most painful question, "Why? Why did this happen to me?" She came up with several reasons. "Maybe he mistook me for someone he hates. Maybe he was drunk and looking for a fight. Maybe I shouldn't have been there. Maybe God is punishing me for being at the gym instead of at home, cooking dinner for my husband and daughter. Maybe God is punishing me for not being as good a wife and mother as I should be."

Wendy was in despair. She believed in God and was strongly influenced by her belief that God had a plan for each of us, lessons he wanted us to learn. "This attack must be a lesson," she concluded. Wendy was utterly immobilized by the enormous implications of the meaning of the assault. It meant she was a bad person, marked by God to suffer. It meant she was a failure as a wife and mother. How could she go on?

Though Wendy's body was healing quite well, it was obvious that she was deeply depressed. She barely ate, her sleep was wracked with nightmares, and she hardly spoke. When she did speak, she mumbled apologies to God and made promises to do better. Her husband and daughter were puzzled by all the religious references, but they said nothing about it. They thought a few more days of rest in the hospital would be good for Wendy, and her doctors agreed. When Wendy was told about the extended stay, the color left her face and she asked aloud when God would stop punishing her. The dark cloud she saw hanging over her head would probably never go away.

How We Explain the Unexplainable

Wendy's terrible experience led her to do what we all do when something significant happens—seek an explanation. Un-

---

▶▶ **TAKE ACTION** ▶

Face Your Devil

Each person's depression has a face of its own. Nobody but you can identify the demon that plagues you. It often helps if you face this monster for what it is, instead of avoiding confrontation with the mysterious villain in your psyche.

Use colored pencils or crayons to draw an image of your depression experience. Does it look invincible, or can it be overcome? Write a brief story about its conquest.

---

fortunately, she settled on one that involved punishment from God for her perceived shortcomings. Wendy blamed herself, devalued herself, and reduced her self-worth. When your interpretations of life experiences lead you to be harsh and unforgiving with yourself, depression is sure to follow.

Wendy shows many symptoms of depression arising from symbols—destructive thoughts, recurring nightmares, bothersome images, and self-designed explanations for the meaning of depression. Probably most people think about their depression in a symbolic way. Some see it as a black cloud engulfing them, as Wendy did; others say they feel trapped in a cage or that they're being chased by a vicious animal or being publicly humiliated.

The meaning or the form *your* depression takes is your own unique way of relating to it, and it may play a big role in the treatment process. Obviously, a depression viewed as a punishment from God calls for a different approach than a depression simply seen as a rain cloud. Which one do you think would be easier to overcome?

Jim Is Jailer for Himself
The Emotional Dimension

The desert in full bloom had always been Jim's favorite place to go on his vacation. "Lord knows I need to get away more than ever," Jim reasoned to himself, trying unsuccessfully to build some enthusiasm for this trip. His mind spun back to review the last eight months. He knew Marcy had been unhappy with him at some level; she sort of shuffled around the house with that defeated look Jim hated. He was withdrawing from her and taking his frustration out on her two young children. "I should never have gotten involved with a divorced woman with children," Jim said to himself. "I should have known better."

While he absentmindedly finished loading his truck with camping supplies for the weekend, Jim recalled Marcy's parting words after their last argument, and they hurt as much now as they did then. After his gut-wrenching divorce from Bobbi years earlier, Jim suffered alone horribly. He had done nothing but go to work and come home—depressed and hopeless about any future joy. Jim would never again make a relationship—even a single friendship—work. In his own eyes, Jim was an utterly useless human being. Then for some reason, Marcy had reached out to him. And much to his surprise, Jim found himself in a relationship again.

At work, Jim avoided others quite successfully. When he heard the others laugh and tell jokes, he sometimes cried because he couldn't find anything funny in their stories. Often he got angry at how superficial such people were and how insensitive they were to his suffering. Didn't they know he was in emotional pain? Didn't anyone care enough to help him? Why were they happy when he was so miserable?

Jim needed this vacation. He knew he must try to ignite the life spark in himself again, or he'd just give up totally and fade away forever. These last eight months were killing him. He didn't care about anything anymore. When he was reprimanded by his supervisor for declining work performance, he felt even worse when he realized he didn't care about the reprimand. He felt like saying to his boss, "Sorry, but you've obviously mistaken me for someone who gives a damn," but he couldn't do more than think it. He wished the idea amused him, but it didn't. Nothing did.

Packing the truck with supplies fatigued Jim. He felt sad to be going by himself and briefly considered not going at all. Sometimes he could really drive himself crazy with how he felt one way one minute, and the opposite the next. Go camping or stay home—or die.

With a push from someplace inside, Jim climbed into the truck, started it up and left. Again he tried to convince himself he was going to have a good time in his favorite place, and for a fraction of a second he almost believed it.

Hours later, Jim did everything just right to build a comfortable campsite. He scanned the vast horizon and saw no evidence of another human being. Just cactus, desert shrubs, and a dark, clear night sky with an unbelievable number of stars to gaze at. Jim took his rapid fill of the remarkable sight and promptly became even more depressed because being there didn't make him feel any better. "If this doesn't help, *nothing* will." The thought scared him, and he felt even more hopeless than before, when a part of him still hoped the desert would cure his pain. Jim made a small fire and cooked some food. After eating, he sat and listened to the silence. Then he thought, "If something were to happen to me here, it would be a long time before anyone found out about it."

Mood Disorder to the Max

The intense emotional suffering that characterizes depression is the chief reason for its official designation by the mental health profession as a mood disorder. Jim clearly showed all the worst symptoms associated with depression—ambivalence (mixed feelings that prevent you from moving forward in life), no sources of gratification, lost sense of humor, feelings of inadequacy, no emotional attachments (apathetic or uncaring about things), sadness, excessive guilt, anger, no motivation, inability to experience

---

Rule Your Reactions

→ **LOOK DEEPER**

Do you think it's possible for people to pay too much attention to how they feel? When, if ever, is "get in touch with your feelings" bad advice? For example, if you focus on how you feel about standing in line at your bank, does that really enhance the experience?

---

pleasure, feelings of powerlessness and hopelessness, and low self-esteem.

This kind of intense emotional suffering leads people to thoughts of suicide. None of the suicidal people I ever treated really wanted to die; they all just wanted to escape the pain of living. What you need to know is that things can and will get better. And when they do, you really should be here.

Henry Can't Stand People— People Can't Stand Henry
The Relational Dimension

Henry sighed and took one last look at his drawings. Satisfied his client would be happy with this architectural triumph, Henry rolled up the plans, placed them in a cardboard tube for safekeeping, and carefully placed the tube in its own corner of a rack that held at least half a dozen other such tubes.

When Henry opened his office door, the smell of bacon from this morning's breakfast still lingered in the air. Alice had already left for the day, and neither of their teenage daughters was home. He didn't know where they were, and he felt a little guilty that he didn't much care. "Well, they never did talk to me much, anyway," he thought. "They've always been Alice's daughters more than mine."

This was one of those times when working at home was a disadvantage. Finishing an important project in midmorning created a sense of completion that made it difficult to launch right into another project. "No one is home, and the silence is so nice I think I'll just enjoy it awhile." Henry loved solitude the most. Having Alice and two normal (therefore rambunctious) teenagers around all the time had grown tiresome long ago.

Henry didn't feel that he could talk to them about anything important. They were all terribly superficial and paid much too much attention to trivial things. Henry wished they could see the depth of life as he could, but they seemed infinitely more interested in home decor and fashions. How he wished they could share his insights into philosophy and politics or his experiences exploring higher states of consciousness! But as soon as he mentioned any of these subjects, his magic worked—Alice and the girls disappeared; most people disappeared. It had always been that way, if he was honest with himself about it. All through his life, from grade school to college, Henry had been considered the odd one. While others played and socialized, Henry read books by obscure European writers on subjects even more obscure. To Henry, other people were a mystery.

Somehow, Alice had been attracted to this quiet, pensive man. Henry was awkward in his responses to her interest, but Alice was gentle and persistent and eventually won him over. Henry couldn't have known that part of Alice's agenda was to get him to lighten up so she'd have a more complete husband. But she had given up long ago, allowing Henry to slip into becoming the deep and one-dimensional recluse he was now. True, she avoided real contact with him, and she knew this frustrated him. But for Alice it was a necessary act of self-preservation; otherwise she'd get trapped in the deep space of Henry's soul.

Henry sat in the living room and looked around his house. He lived here in every sense of the word. He worked here, read books here, balanced the family budget here, and spent what little real leisure time he had here. Henry rarely went out, except to pick up or deliver building plans or to attend the unavoidable meetings with clients.

Long ago, Henry had established in his own mind that he was a loner. He convinced himself that it was an acceptable thing to be, but he had doubts about that. Other people held no appeal for him. Even those who were well educated and led sophisticated lives invariably surprised him with their superficial attitudes.

If he had to go to a party (for reasons related to the job, of course), Henry would search for someone like himself, willing and able to discuss the complexities of life. But it always turned out the same. He would interrupt the superficial pleasantries people were exchanging and turn the talk to something he considered more substantial. Occasionally, he'd get polite interest, but always the deep conversation would dwindle, returning quickly to the mundane.

Many times Henry had tried to make friends. It would be nice, he thought, to have some good friends, but it just never happened for him. Henry sometimes wished he could be superficial like everyone else, but most of the time he saw loneliness as the price for having a superior intellect.

Henry began to resent the time he was spending thinking about his lifestyle. He abruptly decided that other people were simply not worth the time and energy they took for what little they could contribute to his life. He went to the bookshelf and scanned it for a book to read. He finally settled on Ayn Rand's *The Virtue of Selfishness*.

The Price of Henry's Alienation

Henry's solitary world is an example of the powerful role relationships play in shaping our self-image and mood. Henry shows the inner conflicts and other stresses of one who is uncomfortable alone and with others. He is socially withdrawn and isolated; although he often wishes to have contact with others, he is socially apathetic. He is highly critical of others, finding nothing redeeming even in those closest to him. (Imagine his impact on his daughters' self-esteem! Hopefully, they will learn not to blame themselves for their father's limitations.) Henry has a very narrow range of communication skills, precluding a genuine sharing of personal feelings and insights. He is so rigid in his style that despite years of rejection, he has yet to learn what it takes to build a relationship with another person—including how to survive the transition from superficial first contacts to deeper bonding over time.

Beyond the poor relational skills that are proving hurtful to Henry, other symptom patterns on this relational dimension can lead to or maintain depression. Perhaps the most common of these is to evolve a victim demeanor; you put yourself at the mercy of the other person's wishes instead of operating as an

---

▶ TAKE ACTION ▶

Give Your Version of Interpersonal Skills

If an alien from another planet landed on Earth and asked you to explain how human beings relate, what would you say? Make a list of the elements that make up good interpersonal skills, and explain each one in terms of real behavior. Here are a few to get you started in describing good interpersonal skills.

Skill	Associated Behaviors
Attentiveness	Making eye contact Listening without interrupting
Honesty	Stating facts despite self-incrimination Stating facts despite negative feedback Giving an accurate representation of circumstances
Warmth	Having a welcoming attitude; smiling; touching Being nonjudgmental Making statements of appreciation and acknowledgment

equal. Likewise, if you are highly dependent on someone else and unable to provide well for yourself, then you are in a pattern that invites victimization. Another common pattern is to seek approval from others to the point where you let them take advantage of you. Finally, acting in the manner of a martyr may mean you are taking too much or too little responsibility for others' thoughts or actions.

The relationship dimension is often at the heart of depression. Feeling trapped in a bad relationship, getting rejected by a loved one, being excluded from the closeness of a good relationship, suffering the death of a dear one, seeing that you are a turnoff to others whose acceptance or approval you want—such issues are among the most emotionally charged situations we encounter. The result is that they become potential sources of depression. Learning to manage relationships well is *vital* to defeating depression and preventing its return.

Anne, the Queen of Negativity
The Thought (Cognitive) Dimension

Anne did her typical stumble out of bed. She elected not to look in the mirror while she brushed her teeth because she was sure she wouldn't like what she saw. She was pretty sure her eyes were conspiring to form supportive bags. Worry did that to her. (Her family and friends used to kid her about how they could always tell when something was wrong in her life just by checking for "the bag sign," as it came to be known.) Anne never liked her eyes anyway, but she especially hated their transmitting secret messages she couldn't seem to contain.

Wearing a grubby robe, Anne self-consciously stepped out onto her porch to get the morning paper. After searching for it for several annoying seconds, she saw the paper trapped in a bush beside the driveway. She was sure the delivery boy had thrown it there just to aggravate her. Anne thought she must be a magnet for abusive people. Cashiers would shortchange her in the grocery store; drivers would cut in front of her on the road; service people would show up late. She felt such people were always taking slaps at her for one reason or another, and it frustrated her to tears sometimes, not knowing the reason. She could only conclude that she must be a pretty worthless person to be treated this way time after time.

She took the paper inside and sat down with it at the kitchen table. She sipped some juice as she flipped pages, looking for the Help Wanted section. Mostly Anne felt as if it were a waste of time to look again, but it was the responsible thing to do. She had looked every day for the last three weeks, since learning that her previous position was not renewed in the company's annual budget. She was always being passed over in one way or another, or so it seemed. Sure, she had her own house, no small feat for a single woman. And yes, it was nice that she had a new car and a loving family and a wonderful boyfriend and a healthy savings account, but . . . well, none of it mattered, because right now she needed a job. She had never been unemployed for more than a month, and even now had a very promising job offer pending. No matter, though. Everything in her life was terrible because every day started with an insensitive paperboy and a Help Wanted section.

Something caught Anne's eye and caused her to look more closely. A new job listing, and for once it actually sounded like something! There was a fraction of a second's excitement, which was immediately quashed by the flow of negative predictions. "I'll never get this job. I'll bet they already hired someone and the listing is to avoid violating any laws. They won't hire a woman for this job. I'll never even get an interview." Anne hesitated for a moment. She wanted to call for information but figured it wasn't worth the bother, since she wouldn't get the job anyway. An hour later, Anne was still at the kitchen table trying to decide whether to call the number in the ad. Meanwhile, she ate several breakfasts as she pondered the unfairness of life.

In a surprise moment of optimism, Anne called the number. A suspiciously pleasant woman answered the phone. When Anne stated the purpose of her call, she felt a twinge of relief when the woman, still pleasant, asked a few questions about her background and abilities. Anne understated her case deliberately, seeing no reason to push. After a few minutes, Anne was asked to set up an interview time. She hesitated, then agreed. Anne hated herself for that little hesitation; still, she did it all the time.

The interview would be later that same day. Anne was thankful for that, lest she have too much time to think about it and back down.

She showered and went to pick out something to wear. She pulled out no less than a dozen outfits, carefully considering, then rejecting, each one. Today was a little worse than usual. Normally, it *only* took her 15 minutes to decide what to wear. Finally, she found something less intolerable than the rest and put it on. Realizing she'd spent valuable organizing time looking for clothes, Anne shifted into high gear, grabbing a resumé and her purse. She raced out the door, brushing her hair as she hurried along. In the car, she put on makeup and perfume as she drove, a talent she had perfected over the years. No near-accidents today—a good sign, she thought.

She arrived two minutes late and was greeted by the woman who owned that too-nice voice of the earlier phone call. She handed Anne an application form and invited her to sit at a comfortable table in the corner to complete it. Anne sat down and looked around, wondering whether this might be her next place of employment. She couldn't decide whether she would like it or not. She handed in the completed application and was surprised when she was called into the interviewer's office after only a couple of minutes. The interviewer seemed friendly, but Anne felt she was looking right through her. Anne shifted in her chair several times while the interviewer cleared her throat and reviewed her application, then her resumé. She nodded several times, which Ann took as a bad sign. Interviewers always nod a lot before they decide they can't stand you.

After a few questions, some polite exchanges about the job, the company, and the others to be interviewed, Anne gathered herself and left. She felt terrible about the interview. She was sure the woman disliked her, even though she was friendly. Friendliness is just an interviewer's cover. She was sure she wouldn't get the job and became even more depressed than at any point in the last three weeks. Anne wondered how long she could handle the abuse life gave her before she would have to give up. The thought of suicide passed through her mind, but the image of an unattended funeral caused her to reject the idea— for now, anyway. As she drove home, Anne was so preoccupied she didn't notice whether she stopped at the stop signs.

Two days later, Anne got the call. The job was filled; thank you for applying, we'll keep your resumé on file for future reference, good luck. Anne was numb as she hung up the phone.

Anne would never know that the personnel director's niece was hired without even having a formal interview.

Anne's Thinking Style Leaves Little Room for Hope

No dimension of experience influences the problem of depression more than the cognitive. Your thoughts, ideas, beliefs, and perceptions are probably the most powerful factors that underlie depression, simply because *how* you think and *what* you think determine so much of what you do and, therefore, what you experience.

Thinking involves creating meaning, establishing connections between things, and countless other activities associated with shaping our experience. It has been shown beyond any doubt that depressed people tend to make certain errors in thinking (technically cognitive distortions). These errors lead to faulty interpretations, inappropriate reactions, and depression. Can you pick out some of the distortions in Anne's case?

Anne's thinking shows many typical depressive symptoms, including negative expectations leading to a sense of hopelessness ("I'll never get this job . . ."), negative self-evaluation (she could only conclude that she must be a pretty worthless person), negative interpretation of neutral events (the delivery boy threw the paper there just to aggravate her), suicidal thoughts, indecision, a victim mind-set in which she was always the loser, worry and rumination (spinning the same negative thoughts around and around), and focusing only on the negative things in her life to the near exclusion of the positive ones.

Other thought patterns associated with depression include global thinking, where the person tends to think in terms of the big picture and misses important details that would make the picture more accurate. This is one reason why depressed people are so easily overwhelmed. If you think of defeating depression as one big goal, for example, but don't understand that achieving

---

TAKE ACTION

Reframe Your Regrettable Responses

Try to think of a specific situation you know you handled poorly. What specific thoughts led you to handle things as you did? Deliberately correct each of those thoughts, then replay the situation in your mind with a successful outcome. Use pencil and paper for this if it helps to see the thoughts in writing.

How does it change your feeling about each situation when you replay it with a successful outcome? The idea is to approach similar situations in the future with better resources. Use these examples to stimulate your thinking.

Situation	Previous Response	New Response
Interacting with the boss	Passively accepted unfair personal criticisms	Assertively refuse to accept unfair criticisms; focus on issues.
Handling a mail order mistake by phone	Started shouting match resulting in frustration and dissatisfaction	Gather documentation before dialing; explain the problem; stay calm and on task of resolving the mistake.

your goal requires many small steps, it will seem impossible to succeed. Global thinkers know *what* they want but have no idea of the smaller steps it takes to get it. For this reason, I talk a lot about *how* to do things, while I encourage you to think in terms of goals *and* the realistic steps to reach them.

Learning to think clearly—including how to separate what you make up in your head from what is really going on out there in the world—is an essential skill for anyone who is depressed or at risk of depression. Many of the activities in this book teach you to approach situations with a realistic, not depressed, attitude.

Marla Battled Big Odds
The Historical Dimension

Marla sat nervously in the waiting area outside the school psychologist's office. She picked at her nails, pulled on her hair, shifted in her seat, and went through numerous other nervous behaviors. She tried to understand why she was so nervous, particularly since this was just one of many times she had been called down to see Mr. Lawrence. He was kind of strange, but Marla liked him. At least he was nice to her. Not many people were.

Marla hoped she wouldn't cry today. She always got mad at herself for crying, yet she couldn't seem to help it. Mr. Lawrence said she was in pretty bad shape and that some big changes would have to be made if she were to continue in this school. True, she got all failing grades, and yes, she skipped school and stayed home whenever school seemed like too much to handle—which was most of the time. He made her see a real psychologist—the type who talks to you about *all* your problems, not just the ones related to school. She liked that guy, too, but he really didn't seem to know how to help her. He always just had her talk about things that happened to her.

When Marla began to realize that this psychologist felt as powerless to improve her situation as she did, Marla stayed home for a week, just crying and wishing she had never been born. Her mom didn't even know she skipped school that week. In the following week, her mom happened to call the school about a matter unrelated to Marla's school performance. When she found out Marla skipped school, she did what she always did. She yelled at Marla, called her nasty names, told her how much of a bother she was now as always, said how much better her own life would be if Marla would either become a perfect child or leave and bother someone else.

Marla bit her lower lip when she felt the tears start. She hated her mother, and she loved her, too, because, well, because she was her mother. But she really hated Mom for marrying her father, a drunken, mean sailor who never knew the slightest thing about responsibility. He left when Marla was only five, but she remembered plenty from those years—the screaming, the door-slamming, the times she was so afraid she hid under her bed until things quieted down. She remembered seeing her mother's bruised face. She remembered her daddy when he came home, sometimes warm and loving to her, sometimes mean and rejecting. She never learned how to predict whether today would be a yelling day or a hugging day.

Suddenly Daddy was gone and Marla found herself in a new home with another man, and Mom told her to call him Daddy. She couldn't understand. This man yelled louder than her first daddy, and something worse. He hit her. Hard. She told Mom, who always took his side and said she deserved it, even when Marla knew she didn't. Every day Marla wondered whether she would get hit again, or whether she could escape to her room, her only sanctuary. She always felt this terrible knot in her stomach when the school day ended because that meant she'd have to go home. "Life is so unfair, and nobody loves me" was the phrase that ran through Marla's head constantly. Unfortunately, she looked the part, too. She was overweight—a fact that did not escape the boys in her school. She wore glasses and had a mild case of acne, her hair refused to stay put, and her clothes were obviously low-budget items.

She saw Mr. Lawrence for only one reason: He was nice to her. It was a welcome experience. The only other real contact she had with men was with her two daddys, whom she hated for what they did to her life. She knew she'd never be anything important to anybody. No wonder she thought it would be stupid to try learning anything or to try being any better. Mom didn't care what she did as long as she was out of the way, and who else was there to care? That's why Marla decided that Mr. Lawrence was being nice only because it was his job. And that's why she gathered her things and quickly left his office waiting room. It was a useless pretense, Marla concluded. No one ever *really* cared about her, and no one ever would.

Later that night her mother asked Marla whether she'd seen Mr. Lawrence that day. Marla said yes and her mother said nothing. Marla went to her room and after a while, she heard her mother go to bed. She went to her closet, packed a few things and sneaked out of the house.

A week later, Marla's mother received a phone call from the police in a city over 100 miles away. They had found Marla sleeping in the bus station. Her mother tried to figure out when she could clear some time in her schedule to pick up Marla.

Marla Is Missing Some Psychological Essentials

It's easy to understand why Marla is already chronically depressed. She has been neglected and abused emotionally and physically. She has had two rejecting and hostile males in the important father role, and a mother so self-absorbed as to be nearly invisible to Marla. Marla's history explains her current depression and, unfortunately, makes it virtually certain that she will always be at risk for depression.

Typical patterns for this kind of depression include a history of significant losses (loved ones coming and going), painful and uncontrollable events in the past that victimize the person (arbitrary punishments, abandonments, humiliations, abuses of any sort), inconsistent demands (rewarded one day for something that brings punishment the next), and living a survival-based existence that precludes developing more sophisticated and effective ways to meet life's challenges.

Marla is consumed with anger and hate, both for herself and the world around her. It will be quite some time (if ever) before she can learn that there are good and loving people in the world, even though she has never yet experienced them.

If you lack the experiences that provide a sense of well-being, of safety and of personal worth, you are likely to develop life patterns that are hurtful to you. You don't do this deliberately, of course; it happens as a result of your own fumbling efforts to generate good and positive experiences. To defeat depression, you must learn how to do this properly. The first step is to find out what you, as an individual, don't do well or handle skillfully, then to work to improve your abilities.

Focusing on the pain of the past is *not* a solution. It may help you to understand why you are the way you are, but

---

➤➤➤ **TAKE ACTION** ➤➤

Pick Up on Values You Missed

What things were you taught to value or disregard as a youth? What things did you learn about and what things *didn't* you learn about? For example, if you learned to be a good caretaker for others, maybe you didn't learn to take good care of yourself. Make a list of things you did and didn't learn. Keep this list handy, because you'll be adding to it as we go along.

Values I Learned	What Was Overlooked
Money isn't everything.	How to save for emergencies Budgeting skills
Always tell the truth.	Telling white lies to spare the feelings of others

explaining the past or the present does not create the new views or skills you need to manage the future better.

EVALUATING *YOUR* EXPERIENCE OF DEPRESSION

The examples and symptoms in this chapter prove again that depression has many faces and can result from numerous and varied life situations.

It doesn't take all or even most of these symptoms to qualify a person as depressed. Some people have adjusted to their own negative experiences in life and have accepted certain symptoms as so commonplace that they hardly even notice them. For others,

► **TAKE ACTION** ►

Trace Your Stages of Improvement

Go back to the original list of symptoms you associated with depression. Add to the list if you wish, then categorize each symptom as physical, behavioral, cognitive, and so forth. Which of these seems most prominent in your experience? Why do you think this is so?

On a piece of paper, rank each symptom in terms of resolving it on an ascending scale of difficulty, 1–10. Next to each symptom, state *specifically* how you will know when that symptom is coming under control. (If you have difficulty being specific here, it's an indication of why things are not yet improving in your own situation.) Here's a guide for your own evaluations.

Symptoms	Rank	Signs of Improvement
Physical Loss of appetite	5	Resuming regular eating habits
Behavioral Frequent outbursts of anger on the job	2	Rarely flying off the handle at work
Contextual Feelings of sadness on the way home from a visit with mother	6	Can separate from mother more easily after visiting

the symptoms are so immediate and painful that they continually dominate all awareness.

The depth of your depression is only partially determined by the number of your symptoms. It's very much a subjective matter, like the concept of a pain threshold. Some people can endure a great deal of physical pain and rarely, if ever, seek medical service for relief; others seek intervention at the slightest twinge.

Since each person's depression is unique, its treatment must be individualized. You need to identify which of *your* lifestyle patterns make you vulnerable. You can't help yourself unless you aim at the proper target.

Symptoms	Rank	Signs of Improvement
Symbolic Compulsive self-reproach when children do poorly in school	4	Accepting the childrens' lack of interest and inadequate preparation as the cause
Emotional Angry when trying to resolve money arguments at home	I	Following a firm budget plan that settles many disagreements
Relational Intimidated by social situations with business associates	3	Taking coffee breaks that combine business and pleasure to ease tensions
Cognitive Indecisive about accepting a promotion offered at work	7	Gathering objective information for making the right decision
Historical Parental home lacking in displays of affection	8	Seeking out and spending time with people who are openly affectionate

LOOK DEEPER

Can You Spot a Symptom When You See It?

Go through each story in this chapter again, and this time, seek to identify the symptoms as soon as they appear in the thoughts, feelings, and behaviors described. Is it easier to evaluate yourself by consulting the symptom checklist you made earlier in this chapter or by detecting the symptoms in real-life situations? Both styles are included to help you identify your own symptom patterns.

KEY POINTS TO REMEMBER

- Stress is a common denominator in depression.
- Depression takes many different forms and has many different causes.
- Everybody feels depressed, more or less, from time to time.
- Symptoms exist in different aspects or dimensions of experience, each one affecting some part of your lifestyle, though you may not realize it.
- Physical disorders can cause the same symptoms as depression, so it's necessary to have a thorough physical examination to be sure depression, not some other ailment, is the problem.
- Learning to think clearly (the cognitive dimension) and relate effectively (the relational dimension) are critical to minimizing depression.
- Your personal past establishes your lifestyle patterns, but making changes in those patterns for the future is what really counts.

Chapter 3

LEARN TO RECOGNIZE LIFESTYLE PATTERNS THAT INVITE DEPRESSION

In the previous chapter, you learned that depression can take innumerable forms—one for every person affected. In that sense, it is more accurate to talk about depressions than depression. Now I want to introduce you to certain psychological patterns so closely related to depression that you can't expect to defeat depression unless you are thoroughly familiar with them. You need to know when and how these patterns surface, then what to do when they appear.

To some extent, the patterns I refer to occur in everyone. While each person is undoubtedly unique, with a particular background and history, years in practice have taught me that there are certain aspects of human experience we all share. You will learn where your patterned experiences come from and which ones can lead you into depression. Most important, I will show you the specific skills you must develop to defeat depression.

LEARNING WHAT'S EXPECTED

From the moment you were born, society began to shape your life in very powerful and dramatic ways. Countless expectations are placed on each of us regarding how we are supposed to behave. The family, one of many representatives of society, is certainly the most prominent force in shaping our individual experiences and, consequently, our individual personality. Then the larger realm of society communicates its expectations to us— sometimes through specific instructions about how to behave appropriately in a given situation (say no to drugs!), sometimes through implied or indirect suggestions (we would never ask a lady her age!).

Throughout life we are rewarded for doing some things and punished for doing others; we are enthusiastically exposed to certain experiences and gravely warned to avoid others. Likewise, we are taught which subjects are acceptable in general conversation and which are not. All this instruction plays a huge role in how we perceive the world around us.

Think back to the things you were encouraged to do and think about as you grew up, things your family did together, things that were considered important in your household. It will explain a lot about where your particular view of the world came from. For example, when I was growing up, my family placed a strong value on taking lots of trips, traveling all over the country to see various attractions. To this day, I love to travel. I truly enjoy going to new places and seeing new things, so I do it as often as I can.

Now think of those things you were *not* exposed to, things that were never talked about, things that you didn't know even existed until later in life. These are just as powerful (maybe even *more* powerful) in shaping your perceptions. Friends of mine who were not raised with an appreciation for travel don't really understand why I always seem to be on the go and why I'm not content to just stay home for my vacations as they do.

It's true; the things we grow up with are normal to us, natural and unquestioned parts of ourselves. It's the things we grow up *without* that often become main issues in our lives.

We learn the most about what is socially acceptable from the immediate family in our earliest years. Later our contacts expand

Learning the Family Style

→ **LOOK DEEPER**

Every family has its own code of behavior—the degree of courtesy to each other, habits of hygiene, etiquette observances, religious observances, dealing with others, and so many more. Children absorb this style like a sponge takes on water, and it governs their attitudes for a lifetime. What were the rules in your family? What were you taught to value? How did you know what was fit to say or do? How did you learn what *not* to say or do?

to other sources of experience and feedback—friends, other relatives, the media (especially television), school (teachers in particular), religious institutions, and more. In essence, each of us is exposed to many forces that continuously shape our perceptions, feelings, and ideas. In the face of these forces, we develop ways of thinking about and responding to life that will either work for us or against us in the long run.

IS IT WORKING FOR YOU?

Once you learn to identify the patterns that work against you, you can predict the onset of a depressive episode. By that I mean that the thought and behavior patterns you learned growing up as you did contributed to the state of depression that led you to buy this book. So for you to defeat depression, you need to identify the key patterns that brought you to the state of distress you're in, *and* you must develop new patterns that give rise to contentment and healthy self-esteem.

I hope that you are beginning to realize that much of what depression is about is *learned*. Therefore, depression can be *unlearned!* Furthermore, you can *learn* to prevent serious episodes of depression and to manage any episodes you do experience so that they are less hurtful.

I call my view of depression the lifestyle model. It suggests that for most individuals, depression is *not* an illness, disease, or mysterious affliction to be tolerated or targeted by unpredictable medicines. In my view, depression is a by-product of faulty learning.

When I say faulty learning, I am *not* blaming you. I am stating directly that you are the way you are because you learned to be that way as a result of all the socializing forces I mentioned earlier. Your background has led you to develop certain patterns, and that is simply a fact. The past is your past. Neither you nor I can change it. However, there is much you can *learn and do* to change your present and your future for the better. If you take the time, as you are now, to learn all you can about yourself and how to handle life situations appropriately and realistically, your depression can become a thing of the past.

The one aspect of your makeup that is far more significant than all the others is your values. In fact, every lifestyle pattern you have is closely related to your value system. So first I would like to focus on your values as they relate to your inner life. Then we can look closely at each of the specific patterns that seriously influence your experience of depression.

LOOK DEEPER

How Do You "Get" Depression?

What do you think of the idea that for most people, depression is a learned phenomenon? What are the implications of identifying depression as something learned, rather than as a biologically based illness? Does your conclusion on this point alter the way you deal with your problem?

THE ROLE YOUR VALUE SYSTEM PLAYS

The process of socialization goes on for as long as you live. In reality, you never stop interacting with others. However, most experts agree that the role of socialization is particularly significant in the first two decades of life, because that's when your entire value system is developed and integrated.

This is a mostly unconscious but strongly internalized framework you use in forming subjective judgments about, and reactions to, the ongoing events of your life. It is your value system that dictates your responses to every experience you have, evaluating what is normal and not normal, good and bad, right and wrong, acceptable and unacceptable, important and trivial. All of us *must* make judgments about every experience, otherwise we have no meaningful way of relating to that experience. For example, we make a judgment about another person because such a judgment gives us an organized basis (*even though it might be an incorrect one*) for dealing with that person. In short, making judgments is a necessary part of formulating a plan of action.

The role of values in human experience has always been tied more closely to the field of philosophy than to clinical psychology. However, in my opinion, your value system lies at the heart of every experience you have and acts as a filter for it. You use your value system to seek out desirable or familiar experiences and to avoid other types. Based on personal values, you develop certain capabilities that seem important or worthwhile, and you ignore the development of others you perceive as less valuable. This is a simple but significant concept, particularly in light of my view that depression arises from incomplete or faulty learnings. *The things you don't know how to do can and do cause depression,* as you will see from examples throughout this chapter. Ultimately, the basis of mental health is the ability to adapt your skills to the life situations you face.

TAKE ACTION

Chart the Values Society Gave You

Beyond your immediate family, what are the most prominent influences on the development of your particular value system? With pen and paper, create a chart: one column headed "Source," another headed "The Value Taught," and a third headed "How I Express That Value." In filling in these columns, be very specific about where you learned the value, exactly what that value was, and how that value shows up in your everyday behavior and thinking.

As you do this exercise, you will discover that some of these values work very well for you, while others work against you in one way or another. With this information, you can modify your values over time to bring about more satisfying personal life experiences. Here are some examples.

Source	The Value Taught	How I Express That Value
High school English teacher	Accuracy	I carefully check all projects before submitting them to be sure mistakes have been caught.
Supervisor for my first paper route	Dependability	I try to make sure I do what I say I will do, or make contact to explain any delay. I'm careful not to promise unless I'm confident I can deliver.

VALUE EXTREMES

Values seldom exist in the extreme forms. Instead they are held in a range from, say, utter indifference to belligerent fanaticism, with relatively few holding either extreme. Each person has literally hundreds of values, but not all are equally powerful.

List of Values

The following list includes many that play a central role in the depression experience:

1 Achievement vs. simply being
2 Emotional expressiveness vs. emotional containment
3 Being more emotional vs. being more logical
4 Materialism vs. spirituality
5 Being connected to others vs. being isolated
6 Being other-oriented vs. being self-oriented
7 Being task-oriented vs. being people-oriented
8 Being a conformist vs. being an individualist
9 Being competitive vs. being cooperative
10 Maintaining tradition vs. making changes
11 Taking risks vs. being safe
12 Seeking depth vs. seeking variety in experience

Are You Too Other-Oriented?

As you look at the examples above, consider how each one applies to you personally. Think about your own values and how deeply you hold them. For example, look at the sixth value range, other-oriented vs. self-oriented. Obviously, no one is completely other-oriented, nor is anyone entirely self-oriented. Yet it's clear that a person's socialization history can lead to an imbalance on this value range that is too intensely one or the other.

For example, consider the way most women in our country have been socialized. Despite the gains in promoting equal opportunities, most women are still brought up to be other-oriented. Throughout life, mothers advise their daughters to be good children, good wives, and good mothers. Such value-laden advice essentially says, "Your worth comes from what you do in relation to other people, and not from who you are as a unique individual." This value is very different from one that says, "Create and pursue your own independent dreams, even if it means not marrying or having children."

Relate this value to the eighth value of conformity vs. individuality. Suppose a woman is taught to be a good wife and a good mother. To meet that expectation successfully, she would have to conform to a role that she did not create and might not fit her very well. After all, not everyone is good spouse or parent material. If you suppress or override dimensions of your personality to obtain approval from others, your self-esteem lies in the hands of others. It is difficult, if not impossible, to develop a completely healthy sense of self-worth under such circumstances.

Considering the role values play in processing your life experiences, it is easy to see how social conditioning can create

---

▶▶ **TAKE ACTION** ▶▶

How Strong Are Your Values?

Assign a number from 1 to 10, with 10 reflecting maximum belief in that value, to each basic human value in the list on page 59. The more extreme your numbers, the more definite the indication of which values represent your greatest strengths and greatest weaknesses.

patterns that expose you to a variety of negative experiences, including depression. For example, based on what we know about the value that says, "Be other-oriented and conform to the expectations and demands of others" in traditional female acculturation, is it any wonder that women are diagnosed as depressed nearly twice as frequently as men? Here you can see how values like other-orientation and the need to conform lead you to seek out experiences that may, in fact, work against your individual well-being.

The Danger in Achievement Orientation

Each value in the list on page 59 is neutral, neither inherently positive or negative. However, each value is related to many aspects of your life. For example, consider how a typical man in this culture is raised to be achievement-oriented, having been taught from childhood that worth is determined by accomplishment.

It should be no surprise that he has high professional expectations and strives to achieve them, even at the risk of his family relationships. For as long as circumstances permit him to achieve, he can earn great rewards in the form of approval, financial success, professional status, and so forth. But if circumstances change, an emotional crisis may ensue. If this man is somehow blocked from achieving, the central focus of his life is lost. Depression inevitably follows. The significant point here is this: Your values can create rigidities in you that make you a candidate for depression if those values are challenged in some way.

Each value represents an entire way of life. Periods of crisis in a person's life that show up as depression usually occur when a life value system fails, leaving that person unable to deal effectively with the situation at hand. Go ahead—predict the likely outcome for a traditional female who builds her life around others (her husband, her children) who leave her.

When a Value System Fails

Let's consider a woman of 45, married for 25 years, who has raised three children to maturity and met all her standards for being a good wife and mother. How will this woman handle it when she finds out her husband is off to Rio with his secretary? The stability of her world would be shattered. Her entire life was devoted to her husband and family, with little or no experience in meeting her own needs (financial, professional, or social). When her husband leaves, the crisis is acute.

A therapist may advise her to "get on with your life and start to do things for yourself." And such advice would technically be correct; so would advising a depressed person to "cheer up!" But such advice is not likely to help very much. *Not* because the woman doesn't want to change, but because she doesn't know *how* to change. Her life was based on the value that mandated taking care of others, to the exclusion of meeting her own needs independently. Consequently, a history of self-care virtually does not exist for her.

If you study the values list on page 59, it is easy to see how concentrating your efforts at one end of a spectrum can create depressing problems. This is especially so when you realize you can't rise to the values represented at the other end of the spectrum. I call these the "experiential deficits"—imbalances and faulty learnings that are the basis for depression.

You can prevent episodes of depression by identifying your weaknesses (risk factors) for depression, so you can work toward a more balanced approach to living. It is imperative to examine your values to determine the strengths each provides, as well as any associated limitations that may put you at risk later.

If you want to live life fully, you must commit to your values and maintain a lifestyle that consistently reflects that commitment. Depression often arises from situations where we say or do something that violates our own values—how we think we *should* be. To feel good you must learn to acknowledge the value

━━━━━━━━━━━━━━━━━━━━━━━━━➡ **TAKE ACTION** ➡━━

Prepare to Defend Yourself

Go through the values list on page 59 and the relative weight you attached to each basic value in the previous exercise. Now evaluate where your vulnerabilities lie, according to your current lifestyle. For example, if you value achievement and professional accomplishment above all, then you must realize that any interference with your ability to work could create a crisis in your life. Examine your other values and identify specific circumstances relating to each one that pose a threat to your sense of well-being. Doing this helps you decide whether you need to protect yourself from that vulnerability, or whether simply acknowledging it is enough. Choice is better than no choice.

of new experiences as a way to develop a greater degree of emotional flexibility. Maintaining balance in your life means being able to change effectively with the changing times. Previously learned values may have little to do with living life well today. In that case, these values are a hurt, not a help. My credo is this: When what you're doing doesn't work, do something else.

➡ **LOOK DEEPER** ━

Confronting the *Should* Impulse

Consider your gut reaction when you respond to a situation as you think you should, when in reality, you really don't feel that way. I want to emphasize the need to balance your values against the actions you take in managing your life and dealing with people and situations. If you want to feel good, you must know exactly how far you can go in matching your internal beliefs and wishes against the external realities.

OTHER WAYS YOU VIEW YOUR LIFE

So far, I've focused on the role of your values in your daily life. But other patterns also play significant roles in what you experience day to day.

Are You a Concrete Thinker?
Thinking (Cognitive) Style

Each of the cognitive theories of depression I described in chapter 1 emphasizes a stable way of thinking that leads to patterned responses to life situations. Your thinking style can be described in a number of ways. For example, are you an abstract or a concrete thinker? Abstract thinkers are good at conceptualizing and relating to things without having direct experience with them; they're also better than most at sifting out meanings and principles of experience, and they can recognize parallels and similarities in seemingly unrelated or dissimilar experiences. Your mind-set—abstract or concrete—plays a big role in how you see yourself and others. For example, I live in California, where therapists often speak of "sharing energy," "being grounded," "being connected," and "having space." Such phrases have meaning for abstract thinkers but mean nothing to those who require concrete terms and reality-based explanations. Those abstract terms represent ideas more than real experience.

My clients often tell me about goals so vague, so poorly defined, and so abstract that they lack any connection to real life. Those who say they want to "self-actualize" or "discover their essence" are not likely to do well in treatment because there is no real definition of what's supposed to happen. And when a client tells me, "All I want is to be happy," the goal is too poorly defined for me to accept. I need to know: What does *happy* mean to this person? How would he know if he was happy? What would be different? What could he do that he can't do now?

If patterns of abstraction characterize your way of thinking, the absence of concrete and well-defined thought processes represents a problem that would be one focus of treatment. Likewise, if you tend to be so concrete in your thinking that you don't recognize similarities among a variety of experiences, then that inability requires your attention.

How concrete can thinking get? A nurse friend told me this story: A patient she was working with had developed diabetes and needed to self-inject insulin. She demonstrated the technique of injection by using an orange, first penetrating the skin, then delivering the injection. When she saw him again some weeks later, his blood sugar was alarmingly high. She asked if he'd been doing the insulin shots, and he said, "Yes, I've been injecting the orange daily!" Now *that's* concrete!

Some research suggests that in general, depressed individuals tend to be concrete in their thinking style. This shows up when an individual who suffers from a specific problem gets help in solving it, but doesn't know how to use the solution in dealing with other problems that are similar. For example, suppose a person lacks the ability to be assertive in relationships with others. A therapist can provide guidelines and techniques in setting limits in a marriage or some other relationship. When the marriage improves as a result of the plan, the client may put the issue of setting limits aside and totally miss opportunities to use that technique in handling other troubled relationships. This is typical of concrete thinking. I encourage you always to think about how the useful patterns you learn in one situation *might* also apply in other, similar situations.

Do You Think Too Big?
Global Thinking

Another question for you to explore is whether you are a global thinker or a detailed thinker. This involves your ability to break full (global) experiences into component parts and vice versa. Metaphorically speaking, do you see only the trees and not the forest (detailed), or only the forest and not the trees (global)?

Depressed individuals tend to be global in their approach to solving life's problems. For example, if you are depressed, you might take all of the problems that exist in your life and combine them into one huge, overwhelming problem instead of prioritizing the individual difficulties and sequencing your problem-solving attempts. Do you catch yourself thinking or saying things like "I can't deal with all this," "My life is a total mess," or "Nothing I do is any good"? If so, you'll know you are working against improvement by getting lost in feeling overwhelmed instead of focusing on solving specific problems. Anytime you feel overwhelmed, it is a strong clue you are in a global mode and need to get more specific and focused.

Global thinking leads to a paralysis of your will and a total loss of your motivation. Instead of working on a problem a little at a time, you're ineffectively attempting to deal with everything all at once. This global pattern surfaces in many ways; procrastination is one. If you find yourself constantly thinking about *all* the things that you have to do, then doing few or none of them, you are thinking globally. That is, you inhibit taking *any* action by feeling that you have to deal with *everything* all at once. Learn to break down your duties into smaller, more manageable portions.

Another example of global thinking is making self-critical comparisons between yourself and others. The success others achieve is the final product of their sustained effort over time. A detail person recognizes and understands the steps necessary to achieve something and can appreciate the work and effort others invest in success. However, the global thinker sees only the finished product, with no concept of the planning and work involved, then feels overwhelmed and depressed at his own lack of success.

The things you want (happiness, success, a good relationship) are possible for you. If you don't know the steps it takes to get them, you must *learn them! Anything you see another person do is doable!*

Therapy so often involves teaching the client how to break global desires—"I want a good relationship!"—into manageable steps such as these:

1 Attend gatherings.
2 Be friendly.
3 Invite a likely partner out for coffee and a chat.
4 Explore common interests and attitudes. If you like what you see, pursue the relationship. Outcome: Enjoy a close, caring friend and confidant whom you see at least once a week. Your relationship is mutually rewarding.

Consider something as simple as going to a wedding party. When you arrive, you have no visible clues to reveal the effort involved in organizing it. Somebody created the guest list, searched for a suitable location, chose the menu, auditioned the band, decorated the room, and arranged the other countless details that go into giving a successful party. And you are enjoying the finished product.

If I asked you to organize a party, the task might seem overwhelming to you. Yet a party is merely the result of progressive steps, each leading to the next, each involving specific and achievable goals. *Clearly, anything anyone else can do is humanly possible!* You may not know how to do it, but that doesn't mean someone who can do it is competent and you are not. This is distorted thinking.

To improve your sense of self-esteem, you need to invest some time and energy in finding out from informed sources what steps are necessary to bring about the result you desire. Not knowing how to do something is quite different from not being able to do it. To overcome your global thinking, decide what you want, then force yourself to develop specific steps in an organized sequence calculated to get it. If you don't know how to do something, learn from someone who does know and can explain in detail how to do it. If the person has the ability but can't teach you to do it, find someone who *can* teach it. Often, people who have the finest abilities don't really know *how* they

━━━━━━━━━━━━━━━━━━━━▶ **TAKE ACTION** ▶━━━

See How Clever You Are

Think of five activities you are absolutely certain you do well. Create a flow chart that identifies every step involved in performing one of those activities so an inexperienced learner can duplicate the process. Are you surprised at how many steps are involved in doing what you do so well? How clearly can you identify each step necessary to perform the sequence correctly?

do what they do. You learn best from people who can be specific about what they do and how they do it.

Another aspect of the way you think—your attributional style—is characterized by the way you describe or explain why both bad and good things happen to you in life. But it is attributions about bad experiences that lie at the heart of depression. If you blame yourself—that is, respond in a global way—and believe your circumstances cannot change over time, depression is likely to follow. On the other hand, if you limit your conclusions to the one specific situation at hand and recognize that external circumstances also influence events and can change, you are far less likely to experience depression. This highlights the importance of recognizing whether something is in your control and how much it will affect your life.

Focus Your Wandering Mind
Attentional Style

The internal state of agitation and anxiety, so often a part of depression, is among its most troublesome aspects. If you find that you can't maintain a meaningful level of concentration, you must take steps to improve that skill. For example, as you read this book, is it difficult for you to stay focused and remember what you just read? If so, it is obvious that your attention span has been affected by your depression. No, you are not losing your mind, and no, you are not hopeless. But you do need to work on your anxiety or on the jumbled thoughts that are disrupting your ability to concentrate.

Some people use antidepressant medications to reduce agitation and enhance concentration; other options exist as well. You can choose from a variety of techniques, such as hypnosis, meditation, visualization, and guided fantasy, as a way to focus your wandering mind toward a specific direction.

Do you have a negative reaction to hypnosis? If so, you probably have misconceptions about it, since hypnosis is nothing more than relaxing and focusing on meaningful and helpful ideas. Contrary to a common misconception, hypnosis *enhances* rather than diminishes your sense of control. A qualified professional who uses hypnosis can teach you to increase the amount of focused time and, with it, your ability to relax and manage your anxiety. Improved sleep and added energy are virtually sure to follow.

> **TAKE ACTION**

Teach Yourself to Relax

Obtain a relaxation tape from a local bookstore, tape center, or library and practice relaxing with it. If you don't like the tape after playing it once or twice, try another. (Some tapes are really quite good, but the quality of others is poor.) Practice taking the time to sit quietly and relax at different times throughout the day. Notice how your ability to relax and focus on the tape improves with practice. Learning to sit quietly and focus on positive ideas can be a wonderful source of good thoughts and good feelings.

Trying to help yourself is difficult when anxiety or an internal focus on distress impairs your ability to learn effectively. This is when self-management skills for handling anxiety and internal agitation would be of great use to you. Furthermore, these skills work to reduce the potential for negativity and stress when practiced regularly.

Use Every Part of Your Nature
Self-Acceptance

A basic truism in psychotherapy is this: "The harder you try to control a part of yourself, the more that part controls you." People who feel depressed and lack control of their lives tend to label parts of themselves negatively for a variety of reasons, and then try to get rid of those parts. For example, I recently treated a woman who seemed to be one of the sweetest, kindest, gentlest souls you could ever meet. She reported that she was that way most of the time. But every few months, for no apparent reason, she would throw a major temper tantrum, sometimes endangering her family by throwing things, even physically assaulting them.

This woman's background placed a strong value on being sweet and good and devalued the expression of other basic emotions, particularly anger. In essence, she labeled the angry-feeling part of herself as bad, and she invested enormous amounts of energy in suppressing any angry feelings that rose up in her. So instead of recognizing and accepting anger realistically as an emotion basic to all people (herself included) and learning to deal with it appropriately, she suppressed her anger until it reached a level so intense that she could no longer contain it. Then it would surface in dramatic and powerful ways.

Whenever you label a natural part of yourself (anger, sexuality, appetite, jealousy, competitiveness, insecurity) as bad and attempt to get rid of that part, you deny a basic element in yourself, and you are destined to fail. If you try to eliminate your appetite for sweets, you're likely to chuck it all in regular eating binges; if you try to suppress your sexual feelings, chances are that they will surface eventually in irresponsible sexual actions. The point remains the same: Any attempt to suppress natural parts of yourself is destined to fail.

A far more realistic response is to accept the reality of such parts and investigate their purpose and value. Anger, for example, is a basic and necessary emotion that can lead you to defend yourself, set limits in your dealings with others, motivate positive action, and give vent to frustration—so its positive potential is obvious. However, it is not necessary to throw destructive tantrums and abuse others. Once you accept the inevitability of angry feelings, your task is to recognize anger in its earliest stages (simple irritation or annoyance, for example) and respond to it in a sensible way.

The need to accept and make good use of all of your parts is fundamental to managing your life in a responsible, satisfying manner. The goal is not always to change yourself; sometimes you must work to put yourself in situations where your natural characteristics are recognized as valuable. For example, if you're a free spirit, this aspect of your nature makes you shine as an artist or a teacher of preschoolers; but joining the Army as a free spirit is dangerous for your self-esteem. You have to pick your shots, giving yourself the best chance to use your gifts for success. Realistically identify your assets and liabilities, then try to figure out which environment will be most supportive of your needs and most appreciative of your talents.

Look at the Broad Picture
Perceptual Style

Depressed people tend to magnify their bad experiences and minimize their good ones. A depressed individual's view of any experience is usually a distorted one. The tendency to "catastrophize"—make small annoyances into major setbacks— illustrates one of the cognitive distortions outlined by Aaron Beck, M.D., that can cause serious discomfort. Then, when you learn to put things into perspective, you begin to recognize that your feelings are too intense for the situation at hand. You see how important it is to get some distance and break things into manageable pieces.

Another aspect of perceptual style is selectivity, the equal opportunity you have to see good alongside bad in every situation. To notice only the bad or only the good is to distort perception.

A key point here is that perceptions can be distorted by choice, for better or for worse. So whenever possible, it is necessary to seek objective information. Any depressed individual who distorts information in a negative direction actually fuels his depressed feelings. That's why it is important to seek objective information so you can discount any automatic negative interpretations you make.

Far too often, depressed individuals get so caught up in their own negative ideas and negative frames of reference (including negative interpretations and negative expectations) that they stop responding to the external realities. Consider the person who repeatedly attempts to get the approval of a parent who continuously withholds it. If you try, try, and try again to get your mother's approval, continually doing things *you think* will please

---

→ LOOK DEEPER

Can You Deal with External Realities?

Why do you think people respond so much more to their internal feelings and desires than to external realities? What impact do you think the field of psychology has had on general awareness? What's the effect of the frequently promoted idea "Where there's a will, there's a way"? Are you skilled enough at reading people and situations to keep from getting caught up in situations that might prove harmful to you?

her, that effort is an example of what I call internally generated experience. It does *not* let you relate to your mother in a way that allows you to ask the most important questions: "Is Mother even capable of expressing approval? What, if anything, does Mother value in terms of my capabilities that would get her to give approval?"

As you can see, it is extremely important to go outside yourself so you can view the situation realistically before you concentrate on some unrelated goal you created internally. In truth, what goes on in your mind may be *irrelevant* to what's going on in the real world.

Who's in Charge Here?
Locus of Control

Your idea of where the control lies in a given situation is strongly related to how you feel in that situation. As Martin Seligman's model of learned helplessness suggests (see chapter 1), if you feel victimized by circumstances, depression is likely to follow. On the other hand, if you think you have some control over a situation, the likelihood of becoming depressed is reduced. The feeling of being victimized by circumstances is called an external locus of control; the feeling of being in control of a situation is called internal locus of control. In general, developing and maintaining an internal locus of control, in which you can make choices and act on those choices, effectively minimizes episodes of depression.

Being unclear about the issue of control can result in attempts to control things that can't be controlled. Or you might pass up an opportunity to take control when you really could. Learning to judge accurately whether a situation you face can be controlled is a skill vital to anyone who wants to respond effectively to life's daily events. The locus of control is an essential concept that gets more detailed consideration in chapter 6.

LOOK DEEPER

Meditate on the Mystery of Control

Why is it so important to some people that they be in control of every situation, to the point that they are willing to brutally dominate others to achieve that control? Why do other people give up control so easily?

See What Time Means to You
Temporal Orientation

Everybody forms a relationship with "time." How you do it is also a learned pattern. Some people are taught to value tradition intensely, and that encourages a strong relationship to the past, called past orientation. Others are taught to set new goals and continually strive for them, to live each day with an eye on the future; theirs is a future orientation. Those who are bombarded with daily duties focus all their attention on just getting by or on the philosophy of living in the now, a present orientation.

Most depressed individuals have a past temporal orientation and repeatedly focus on what was. They continually review past hurts, past failures, and past regrets. And those who use the past as the reference point for thinking about the present and the future only extend past hurts into the now and later. Unless you understand, deep down, that the future does not have to be merely a reflection of the past, you are bound to have only negative expectations for the future.

The ability to envision positive changes for the future is so grossly impaired in some people that it leads to the most serious problem associated with treating depression, namely suicide. Those who are suicidal have the distorted idea that their current painful experience is a preview of what the future holds. From that perspective, suicide probably seems like a rational alternative, since all that remains is more pain. They don't want death; they just want relief.

It is imperative to realize that if you learn specific skills and interrupt existing patterns to develop new ones, the future won't be just a continuation of the past. Your magnificent mind allows you to imagine and eventually bring about things that do not yet exist. Obviously, I believe deeply in the capacity for people to change, or I would not do what I do for a living, nor would I write this book about your potential for change.

How can you hope to move forward if you keep looking backward? Learning to develop positive expectations for the future is vital for overcoming the hopelessness so common in depression. Don't let your link to the past or present cloud your vision of the future. I will show you how to create a positive future for yourself in the very next chapter.

Learn about Damage Control Compartmentalization Skills

The ability to separate different aspects of your experience from one another is an important skill in maintaining good mental health. This is called compartmentalizing. For some people, experiencing a hurt or a disappointment has a profound effect on every aspect of who they are, while others limit a hurt or disappointment to one part of their lives. If you can compartmentalize effectively, you keep the hurt from intensifying.

One depressed young man I saw not long ago reported to me that he sometimes got into arguments with his live-in girlfriend in the early morning, before each of them left for work. Although the arguments were seldom about anything important, they upset him so much that he sometimes called in sick and spent the day thrashing about in bed. In short, this fellow worked himself into a frenzy over petty arguments. The fact that these small issues triggered such a strong reaction was a sign of his poor ability to compartmentalize. His girlfriend, on the other hand, easily separated her personal life from her professional life, effectively closing their arguments out of all the other things that defined her day.

For most depressed individuals, the early morning is the most difficult time. Once they initiate some positive action, the rest of the day runs on that momentum, getting easier and easier, so that by evening, they usually feel better. What's interesting is how some depressed individuals report to me that mornings are the most difficult (high compartmentalization), while others tell me that a difficult morning ruins the *entire* day (low compartmentalization). Can you distinguish the differences between a bad morning and an entire day ruined? Can you separate different aspects of your experiences so that one bad interaction with someone doesn't ruin your entire day, or one bad feeling doesn't trigger a whole depressive episode?

Learning to separate different portions of your experience is an important skill for you to develop, since your ability to separate distorted thoughts or distorted feelings from your actions is vital to your defeating depression. In effect, you compartmentalize them so you can respond effectively to the situation at hand.

➡ **TAKE ACTION** ➡

Know When to Dismiss Your Feelings

A psychologist's telling his patient "You need to get in touch with your feelings" is almost a cartoon cliché. I believe that at times, it is important for you to get *out* of touch with your feelings.

With pen and paper, identify as many specific situations as you can where it would be to your advantage to get out of touch with your feelings. For example, a good time to get out of touch with your feelings would be during an audit by the Internal Revenue Service, so you could spare yourself the experience of anger or fear.

While most of my colleagues still emphasize the importance of getting in touch with your feelings, I advocate that you learn specific times when to get *out* of touch with your feelings! To make the right choices about being in or out of touch with your feelings, you must know how to compartmentalize different aspects of your daily life.

Of course, it is possible to overcompartmentalize experience, and any such imbalance represents a potential hazard. Some people are so intensely focused on handling things logically that they lose touch with their feelings. The goal is always balance. Balance in the ability to compartmentalize creates the option of getting into or out of a particular type of experience.

SELF-ASSESSMENT OF SIGNIFICANT PATTERNS

It bears repeating that you develop one aspect of your experience at the expense of others. Now you can better appreciate my emphasis on deliberately creating experiences that can provide balance. When your inability to perform a task causes you pain, you must master that task if you are to function in a healthy and balanced way. When your depression stops being a mystery to you, it's because you recognize the patterns in yourself that bring you down. Many ideas for creating such growth-oriented change appear throughout this book.

As your awareness of how you organize experience increases, you will recognize where imbalances exist in your life. Then you can take meaningful steps to broaden your experiences as a way to overcome any existing depression and prevent recurrences as well. Consider this: If you recognize that you are too dependent on others in general, or on one person in particular, that dependency is an accident waiting to happen. If you need other people around, to the extent that you are uncomfortable alone, you are always at risk for an acute depressive reaction if whoever you depend upon should become unavailable to you.

KEY POINTS TO REMEMBER

- Lifestyle patterns either lead you to manage life well or put you at risk for depression.

- Your socialization history determines the range and quality of the lifestyle patterns you develop.

- Your value system is the single most important factor in determining your thoughts, feelings, and behaviors.

- Your value system creates weaknesses that represent risk factors for depression.

- Your thinking style dictates the range and quality of your perceptions and may be described as abstract, concrete, global, or detailed.

- Attentional style is another pattern that determines your ability to focus on meaningful ideas.

- Self-awareness and self-acceptance are necessary if you are to place yourself in situations that bring out the best in you.

- Depression leads to selective perceptions that amplify the negative. It's important to amplify the positive in your awareness.

- Perceptions regarding control dictate whether you see yourself as a victim or master of experience. Being a victim is a reliable path to depression.

- Temporal orientation refers to your relationship to past, present, or future experiences. To preoccupy yourself with past hurts diminishes your ability to focus on future positive possibilities.

- The ability to compartmentalize is necessary if you are to address different areas of your life effectively, without conflict.

- Any imbalanced (extreme) pattern puts you at risk for depression. The goal is to develop balance, realizing each part of yourself more fully.

━━━━━━━━━━━━━━━━━━━━━━ ➤➤ **TAKE ACTION** ➤➤ ━━

Do You Fit the Patterns?

Go through the patterns in this chapter and identify in very specific terms how each one relates to your styles of thinking, feeling, and behaving. See where you can clearly recognize imbalances. Recall as many experiences as possible to show that the pattern really reflects on how you do things.

Now here is an opportunity for preventive action. Your serious discomfort in being alone emphasizes your need to work at being comfortable alone. Rather than diminish the worth of other people in your life, this ability redefines your relationship to them as an equal, not a dependent. Also, note any patterns you observe in yourself that diminish your ability to function fully. Then you can make a plan to target them for development.

The patterns described in this chapter are vital in organizing your experience. Consider each as it applies to you individually, thinking carefully of the areas you excel in and those where you are most vulnerable. This suggests where you can focus your efforts to regain balance and overcome depression. It also suggests important ways you can minimize the risk of future episodes.

Chapter 4

SEE WHY YOUR PAST IS *NOT* YOUR FUTURE

When I came out to my waiting room, I was immediately struck by the sight of my new client, Mel. A physically large man—very tall and remarkably obese—Mel dwarfed his wife, Betty, who sat next to him with her arm linked in his. Mel's eyes were closed, and he did not open them when I introduced myself and extended my hand in greeting. Betty took my hand, and the look in her eyes told me volumes about her struggle. She politely introduced herself, then Mel, who made no move to acknowledge my presence. His deliberate refusal to recognize my being there was a powerful indicator of Mel's emotional pain.

Getting him to stand up and follow me into my office was only the first of many challenges to come. Betty stood first and gently pulled on Mel's arm in a nonverbal command to stand. After a while, he did. I wondered how she managed to get this huge man out of the house and to my office. I watched Mel closely, waiting to see when he would open his eyes to find out where he was going. He never did.

Betty nudged him along and led him slowly to a large arm-chair in my office. Again, she signaled Mel to sit. He fell grace-lessly backward into the chair, with his eyes still closed. Here was this deeply troubled man I was supposed to help, and he had yet to make a sound or establish eye contact with me!

BETTY TELLS MEL'S STORY

After only a moment, in a tired voice, Betty began an obviously oft-repeated monologue. She described Mel and all he had been through. Watching Mel as Betty spoke, I could not help but notice the steady stream of tears that rolled down his cheeks. I gingerly placed a tissue in Mel's fist; he passively accepted it, but didn't use it. Betty noticed Mel's tears and my little effort to comfort her 60-year-old husband, but she just kept telling Mel's story.

Betty described his serious heart attack of not quite a year ago. He had undergone immediate quadruple bypass surgery, and from the moment Mel woke up after the surgery, his behavior was as I saw it now in my office. He rarely spoke or even opened his eyes. Each day, all day, he sat in a chair at home and cried.

As Betty continued her narrative, I asked questions occasionally, directing them to Mel. But he made no move to answer, so Betty answered for him.

Mel had been seen by quite a few psychiatrists and psychologists, two of them while he was still in the hospital. His unresponsiveness frustrated them all to the point where they withdrew from the case and referred Mel elsewhere. I hoped I could help him.

Betty went on with Mel's history. A hard worker all his life, Mel took great pride in his job as a factory supervisor. He had worked hard ever since he was a teenager, rarely calling in sick, reluctant even to take vacations. His marriage to Betty had been of the stable-but-seesaw type—lots of rough arguments, lots of tender making up. They never even considered dissolving the marriage. Mel had wonderful plans for their retirement, about three years down the line. (They'd take their motor home all over the country at their leisure.) Now, it seemed that their dream belonged to a different lifetime, one totally unrelated to the hell of the past year. As Betty described the retirement plans, Mel moved in his chair, as if positioning himself to say something, but he didn't.

CAN YOU MAKE A DIAGNOSIS?

What do you think is going on inside of Mel that would account for his deep depression? Pause and answer that question before you read on. It's important that you do, because your answer will show how tuned in you are to the main theme of this chapter.

Ready to go on? Did you answer that Mel was feeling sorry for himself, or that he was unable to adjust to the reality of his heart attack? Do you believe he was grieving for the loss of his health or career, or that he was unable to deal with issues of his own mortality? All of these are reasonable ways to explain Mel's depression.

Are any or all of these explanations correct? The answer is "yes, but . . ." But . . . they are not central to what is going on with Mel. One fundamental pattern called future orientation is controlling his experience. A future orientation is the ability to relate to the future as though it were as real and immediate as whatever is going on right now.

You are not born with this ability. You learn and practice it as you mature. Those who have a well-developed future orientation use it automatically, like walking or talking. But this happens *only* if parents or other significant people in your life serve as examples for you and encourage you to develop the ability. They do so by requiring you to plan ahead, anticipate consequences of your actions in detail, and have a variety of specific goals—short-term, intermediate, and long-term. Too few people sense the importance of specific goals because they are caught up in day-to-day living.

Many schools of thought emphasize the importance of the here and now experience, of being present in the moment, of living life one day at a time. These viewpoints are well-intentioned and often quite sensible. However, if you are so caught up in what's going on *now,* you might do things that seem okay at *this* time but will be disastrous later. For example, it's certainly exciting to meet and fall in love (or lust) on a whirlwind weekend—but then to rush off to Las Vegas and get married? The probability that such a couple would still be married in 25 years is slight.

How now oriented can people be? Consider this pattern in the context of the way we treat our planet. How farsighted do we have to be to realize that poison spewing from smokestacks now will eventually harm us all? How much vision does it take to know that destroying the irreplaceable rain forests, at the current rate of 90 acres a minute, will someday have a negative effect on the rest of the planet? Tens of millions smoke cigarettes *now,* never thinking of the harm that can result later.

WHAT YOU CAN PREDICT

Not everything is predictable, of course, but many things are. Future orientation is not an *either/or* characteristic. For example, you can be quite future oriented in your work and be very here and now in your relationships. Without a refined ability to think ahead, life becomes only the present moment, and if the present moment seems terrible to you, depression is far more likely to occur.

Some people are more past oriented. Such clients will tell me they have no idea what they'll be doing next week, but they can recall in great detail every past hurt, including slights at recess in second grade. Too strong an emphasis on the past or the present can cause or aggravate depression. The same is true if you are future oriented or goal oriented to the point of mishandling current situations. In general, though, the lack of a positive future orientation is most likely to be associated with depression.

I believe that imbalances in orientation of any sort open the door to depression. Placing too much emphasis on the past or on the present, for example, leaves the future an underdeveloped dimension. That leads to hopelessness and negative expectations for the future, based on what's going on now or what happened before. The future is much more than just a continuation of the past or the present, but it's all too typical of depressed thinking to see the future only as more of whatever is depressing you right now. Don't let yourself fall into that trap.

This is why I focus your attention on the pattern of future orientation. Rehashing your past does nothing to help you relate positively to the future and all the good things you can bring about. The value of understanding your past is limited and is only worthwhile if it helps you identify the things you must learn to do better. The therapies I do are brief because I don't need to hear the minutiae in the history of my client. How many victim stories does it take for me to realize that a person has yet to learn how to take control of life and make good things happen? The patterns described in the previous chapter are the ones that need your attention. You will discover that the things you do incorrectly or don't know how to do at all are the very things that cause or prolong your depression. You must learn to fill in the

Stopping the Misery Parade   → LOOK DEEPER

Imagine having an unlimited opportunity to tell of hurtful incidents in your life. At what point, if ever, would you decide to stop focusing on the past and start thinking about a different and better future? Be specific about how you would know when the time came to look forward and not backward.

gaps in your experience and initiate more experiences you will find satisfying.

I want to stimulate your thinking about how to develop a positive sense of the future as a tool to defeat depression. I'll provide some activities that will enhance your power to think beyond the moment.

HOW SUICIDE IS TIED TO A SENSE OF THE FUTURE

What does future orientation have to do with suicidal feelings? Plenty. Suicide has been called the permanent solution to a temporary problem. Why do people do it? I've worked with many suicidal people over the years, and it's obvious to me that these people did not truly want to die. Rather, their emotional pain was so great that they felt it was impossible to endure it anymore. Suicide is not a wish to *die*. It's simply seen as a quick way to end the suffering. When such seriously depressed people have the will and courage to develop a plan for a positive future and commit themselves to working at the plan, the suicidal feelings dissipate. What seems hopeless rarely is.

Suicidal intentions are a sure indication of a poorly developed sense of positive future orientation. Anyone who contemplated committing suicide had to anticipate a future devoid of all hope, a future bounded by the same intensely painful feelings of the moment, in the same, or even more hurtful circumstances. Thinking of the future in this way stifles development of positive motivation that comes from wanting to attain worthwhile goals. Wanting to stop the hurt or wanting the depression to go away are *not* goals. They are merely wishes.

If you are suicidal, I assure you that the future holds unlimited possibilities and that it is your current way of thinking that prevents you from knowing it. Because of your depression, you may feel you can't muster the effort needed to make things better. But that may be because you think you have to do it all at once. You don't! Just making the first move on a specific path to improving your future will relieve some of your pain. In fact, you have already made a very good start by reading this book.

Now you must learn to think about the future realistically, something you definitely do *not* do when you're feeling suicidal. I'll show you how to do that in this chapter.

If you feel desperately suicidal right now, first let someone skilled help you to think beyond the immediate pain, so you can experience the relief that is definitely possible. Skip to chapter 10 and *see a professional at once!* Do not let the bad feelings of *now* prevent you from enjoying the good ones that will come later. You can't realize how temporary these bad times are until you're looking back on them later, wondering how you could ever have felt this way.

IS YOUR VIEW OF THE FUTURE DEPRESSING YOU?

Let me get back to that first meeting with Mel, the man I described earlier. The most response I got from him that first day was a grunt or a nod. I knew he was listening, of course, but he couldn't, or didn't want to, expend the effort required to talk to yet another "shrink."

At our second meeting, I left Betty in the waiting room and saw Mel alone. I didn't ask questions or require that he respond to me in any way. Instead, I began to describe some of my clients, their problems, and how their mistaken ways of looking at things caused them pain. I emphasized the common theme of people so caught up in concerns of the moment that they inadvertently made bad decisions for the future. I told Mel about one fellow who dropped out of high school so he could buy a flashy car; I described a young woman who planned to marry a bad risk just to get out of her parents' house; plus lots of other going-nowhere stories. After several of these stories, Mel opened his eyes and looked directly at me for the first time. He said, "I'm going to die." Then he started to sob uncontrollably.

Does that tell you most of what you need to know about Mel? Whatever the details of his life, his depression clearly stemmed from the belief continually spinning around in his mind that his life was over. With no future, in *his* mind anyway, Mel is sitting in a chair, literally waiting to die. Now, if *that* isn't depressing, what is?

If Mel thinks about the future at all, it's overrun with images of his being dead, or nearly dead. He knows his heart is bad, and death can come at any moment. To him, that means he can't go anywhere or do anything because of the unknown (but surely negative) effect it will have on his heart. So Mel sits and waits.

Now come with me into the strange world of depressed thinking. Why didn't Mel's cardiologist assure him that he was fully recovered from the heart attack? He did! But Mel didn't believe him. Why doesn't Mel read the good news about living a normal life after a heart attack? The fact that other people play tennis, take trips, go back to work, and *live* only depresses Mel more. Why? Because *they* may be able to do those things, but Mel is sure *he* can't. Why not explain to Mel that he would reduce the risks of another heart attack by becoming active and eating carefully, rather than sitting around all day and getting fatter? Because Mel *knows* that his number will come up no matter what he does.

MAKE HOPE PART
OF YOUR THINKING PATTERN

Are you getting a sense of how closed the depressed mind can be? Can you relate to how Mel's thinking patterns work against his feeling better? What about *your* patterns? You may remember my brief descriptions earlier of how depression is paired with distorted thinking. One of the most prominent features of depressed thinking is hopelessness—an expectation, a premonition, that the future holds only negative possibilities. You know, I'm sure, how powerfully expectations influence what eventually happens. When you are hopeful, you think things can work out for the better—*in the future*. And they usually do.

Hopelessness is so central to depression that full recovery from depression is highly unlikely for as long as hopelessness remains a part of your thinking. You must learn to think in terms of *positive possibilities* to defeat depression. Thinking about *what can be* (instead of *what has been* or *what is*) is a starting point for becoming a skilled goal-planner. Even in a situation where there is no way out, where you can't change circumstances (a terminal disease, for example), you can work to change your thoughts and feelings about those circumstances.

In most cases, though, circumstances *are* changeable, and we need to change them if we are to escape from the trapped, hopeless-victim-of-life mentality that characterizes depression.

Another aspect of hopelessness that profoundly impacts on the experience of depression involves your style of attribution (explanation of life events), which I spoke of in the first chapter. One dimension of the attribution style is known as *stable/unstable*. Stable reflects an unchanging situation, while unstable situations are changeable. For example, if I believe I will *always* be depressed because I am a loser, my belief is a stable one, predicting that my life will never change. Obviously, I don't have a lot to look forward to.

━━━━━━━━━━━━ ➡ **TAKE ACTION** ➡ ━━

How to Approach the Future

How do you create your ideas about the future? Do you extend the present into the future? Do you imagine only negative things happening (or positive things not happening)? Write about or at least think of an impersonal situation that makes you feel hopeless (pollution, nuclear war, or some such thing). Ask others how they would solve that problem if they had unlimited resources, then if they had only currently available resources.

What did you discover about people's perceptions of available options? Did you find that some people simply gave up before exploring all the possibilities? How would *you* respond?

As you read this, it is probably easy for you to pick out the distortion in statements like "I'll always be depressed" and in the example Mel presents. But unless you become skilled at recognizing *your* specific way of creating hopelessness, you will continue with your current depressed feelings and risk more depression in the future. I want to provide *hopefulness* by encouraging you to identify and correct your beliefs and any attributions that cause you hopelessness and despair. But more than that, you are learning the absolute need for skillfully planning and carrying out positive future-oriented behaviors.

MOTIVATION DEPENDS ON BUILDING HOPE

In the week that President Bush unveiled his multi-billion-dollar strategy for escalating our war on drugs, many news stations made a point of interviewing the youths of America for their reactions. In San Diego, one news station sent a reporter to a drug rehabilitation center for adolescents. When asked what they thought of the president's plan, every single one of the teens in the program expressed, in one way or another, the belief that it was doomed to fail, that drugs would forever be a fact of life in America. The attitude was "Why bother?" None of them expressed any hope that education or increased money or *anything* could improve the situation. Theirs was a "give up and roll over" response. It reflected a lack of motivation even to try when the goal seemed too difficult to achieve.

When you are depressed, almost everything seems overwhelming. Simple tasks seem difficult, difficult tasks seem impossible, and the energy to deal with much of anything—easy *or* hard—is missing. So now, at a time when depression makes you feel anything but ambitious, I am encouraging you to be actively involved with this book. At a time when you are depressed and feel hopeless, I am suggesting that you work at building hope. At a time when your future seems entirely negative or at best uncertain, I am telling you in a firm and deliberate way that your future can be much better than anything you ever experienced. But you need a plan, and a good one, to make it happen!

Why try to move forward with your life when you've been hurt and you feel so bad? Why try harder when you've already tried so hard? There's one strong reason I can think of: What you have done so far hasn't worked. That doesn't mean you can't do what it takes to improve your life. It only means the approach you used wasn't right for the results you wanted. Before you relive the frustration or pain of your failed attempts and give up, why not allow for the possibility that other techniques *can* work and that you can master them! We are taught, "If at first you don't succeed, try, try again." I would add ". . . and when you try, try again, try something *different*."

For you to defeat depression, your expectations must be positive. You must absorb the idea that *change is possible* and that *you can make good things happen in your life* if you approach each situation intelligently and with some flexibility. (Otherwise you might keep doing what doesn't work over and over again.)

A Life Frozen in Time

LOOK DEEPER

If you wanted to keep your life exactly the same as now, how would you do it? What would you do to stay in the same frame of mind, work at the same job, keep the same relationships, the same *everything?* How would you avoid meeting influential new people—become a recluse? How would you stop learning new information—stop reading the papers and watching the news? How would you keep yourself from trying new things—dig yourself deeper into the rut you're in now?

Spend a few minutes creating this scenario in your mind in enough detail to recognize it as implausible. It soon becomes obvious that things *can't* stay the same for you or anyone else. And since things *will* change, your goal is to guide the changes to your advantage.

When your negative expectations lead to a what's-the-use attitude, clearly you must see that some ideas and techniques in this book just might help. This chapter serves as an introduction to the many important strategies against depression that follow in later chapters. *I* know these ideas and methods work, but what basis do you have for hope right now? My word as a professional? Not enough. I want you to think a little differently.

TAKE CHARGE OF CHANGE

If you spent any time on the exercise on page 91, you saw very quickly the absurdity of trying to create a reality where there would be no change. Changes occur no matter what you do. The idea is to control the changes and to deliberately seek out changes that will help you deal with life better. It's not enough just to change; the change must be deliberate and headed in a *specific* direction.

One change for you to seek out involves expectations and future orientation. First you need to realize that motivation ebbs and flows in *all* people. For depressed people, the motivation to change is either buried in a sense of hopelessness or is frustrated by a lack of knowing *how* to make things better.

One way to start making things better is by learning to think beyond the current moment in a realistic manner. Another way lies in learning that changes really *do* occur when you do things differently. As you develop more positive and realistic expectations in your life, self-destructive indifference and lack of motivation will undoubtedly give way to an interest in learning how to achieve your goals.

WHAT DO YOU WANT FOR THE FUTURE?

If I could wave a magic wand and eliminate depression from your life forever, what would you do with your future? Think about it for a moment. Is there something you feel a need to experience, or something significant you really want to accomplish? What is your purpose in life?

That is one of the most profound of all human questions. For some, life is filled with deep meaning and purpose. Others only see life in terms of day-to-day existence, something to get through, nothing to strive for.

Viewing life as purposeful bears directly on the depression experience. For one thing, everyday life can be overwhelming for those who read too much into simple and random events. On the other hand, those who see little if any meaning in life's events may be sacrificing insight into patterns that could prevent or minimize future pain. Obviously, we need to find a balance between thoughtful consideration of what happens to and around us and indifference to what goes on in our lives.

We also need a sense of purpose to provide motivation and the will to endure beyond immediate suffering. I can think of no more gripping example of this observation than psychiatrist Viktor Frankl's experiences in the Nazi concentration camps during World War II, as described in his book *Man's Search for Meaning*. Frankl couldn't help but notice how differently individual prisoners reacted to the brutal conditions. All were starved, beaten, humiliated, and sick, yet some people managed to endure while others quickly died. What made the difference? Frankl's answer was *purpose*.

Frankl himself was separated from his wife at the start of their imprisonment, and he had an intense desire to live so they could eventually be reunited. Notice that Frankl had a purpose, plus the conviction that the current horror would end in time, permitting the longed-for reunion. (His attribution was that conditions were unstable.)

DO YOU HAVE A DRIVING FORCE IN YOUR LIFE?

What drives you? Many of my clients seem to have nothing in them that generates a sense of purpose or meaning. Consequently, they have no future that compels them, no goal that pulls them along. The day-to-day routine is their whole life, rather than only a part of it.

Let me illustrate the point with the case history of a man who came to me complaining of terrible depression. This 40-ish, very successful real estate developer is literally worth millions. I had seen him some months before, when he was experiencing difficulties in his new marriage. Using some of the techniques I taught him, he quickly resolved those issues.

Now he was back, telling me that for the first time in his life, he was comfortable on all levels. He had nothing left to fight for professionally, financially, or personally. He had fought all his life to get to this point. But the need to achieve was a fundamental part of his makeup. When his achieving days were over, depression resulted from a lack of purpose, along with the associated need he had to anticipate new accomplishments.

My goal was to teach him that he could enjoy life even without any pressure to achieve. Do you see how overemphasis on one aspect of life (in his case, achievement) creates a deficit in another (in his case, merely taking life as it comes)? Lifestyle imbalances pave the way for depression.

How do you develop a sense of purpose? You find something you consider important enough to absorb your time and energy. Today's world bulges with important issues in which your contribution can make a difference, but only you can decide which ones arouse your willingness to become involved. You also have to acknowledge that other things in the world are as immediate and important as your depression. I know this is really hard to do. Yet there is no one so powerful and so future oriented as a person with a mission. Explore the possibilities.

ERICA—A CASE OF DISTORTED SENSE OF FUTURE

Erica arrived at my office looking like a model for Saks Fifth Avenue. Impeccably dressed, perfectly groomed, and very, very

---

TAKE ACTION

Your Values at Work

Do you engage in behavior that is consistent with your values, and do you work in a meaningful way to build your self-esteem?

Try to identify a sense of purpose in the people closest to you—family, friends, neighbors, and co-workers. (Use the example below as a guide.) How do their lives reflect it? What about the quality of life for those who don't seem to have a sense of purpose?

Person	Purpose	Behavior That Reflects the Purpose
Mother	Take care of children	Being constantly available to children
		Volunteering time and energy to meet children's needs
Barbara Bush	Reduce the rate of illiteracy in America	Giving public readings for children to spark their interest in reading
		Writing children's stories
		Lobbying for educational programs
		Running public service ads that encourage learning to read at any age

---

depressed. I'll omit the details and just tell you that Erica had lost her job five years before, and soon afterward, an overwhelming desire for motherhood had gripped her. Her husband, Ray, wasn't sure he really wanted to be a father. In any case, he wanted to wait until they were more financially secure. Somehow Erica managed to convince Ray that they shouldn't wait. She became the mother of a son, now four years old.

Erica pressed a monogrammed handkerchief to her face as she spoke, quickly dabbing away the tears. She saw her son as the cause of her depression:

"I wanted a baby so very much that I couldn't think of anything else," she said. "I pushed Ray into fatherhood before he was ready, and I feel guilty about that. But I feel even guiltier about the fact that I am tired of being Bobby's mother!

"I know that must sound awful to you, but I can't help it. When I was pregnant, I felt like a queen. I was in heaven. When Bobby was born, he seemed like a miracle to me. During that first year, I held him every minute. I looked at him lovingly all the time. I was thrilled. I didn't mind that he cried in the middle of the night, and I didn't mind staying at home with him. I enjoyed it. But by the end of his first year, I was already beginning to feel that I'd had enough of Bobby and enough of being a mother. I started to resent Bobby's total dependency on me.

"I couldn't believe I was feeling that way—I couldn't let myself think it, much less talk about it to Ray or anyone else. What would they think?

"And every time Bobby cried or messed himself, I got angrier at him, and hated myself still more for feeling that way. He's a good boy, and I love him, but dammit, I feel trapped and have felt that way for three years. I can't take it anymore. He *was* the cute little baby I wanted, but he isn't little and he isn't a baby anymore. Now he is forever asking questions and acting stubborn as a mule—and he can't sit still for five minutes. I wanted a baby, not a whirlwind. I mostly came here to find out whether it would help me, psychologically, if I had another baby. What do you think?"

IS SHE KIDDING?

Are you cringing at the thought of Erica's having another baby? I hope so, because she illustrates well how the distorted thinking of people trapped in depression leads them to attempt solutions that will undoubtedly make the problem worse. Erica's "solution" is typical of people who tend to make the same mistake over and over again, risking the same terrible consequences. This is the basis for one of my most important pieces of advice: When what you're doing isn't working, *try something else!*

Let's look at Erica's case a little more carefully. Erica loses her job and decides her next career should be that of mother. She envisions a baby, cute and cuddly, that she can feed and water like a pet. Okay, you have to admit that she has a goal, and I've been talking about the importance of goals. So, what's the problem?

The problem is that Erica's vision of the future at that moment of decision about motherhood is terribly unrealistic. She pictures a baby in her arms next year, but she doesn't anticipate the baby's developing into a child of nursery school age, or a nine-year-old who might break windows and refuse to clean his room, or an irritating adolescent who sulks and sasses.

In short, Erica's sense of the future was so limited that she made what I personally consider one of the most important of life decisions—parenthood—in a totally unrealistic manner. It's a pretty well established fact that babies get older, and barring catastrophe, eventually become adults. Why hadn't Erica thought about that?

BE REALISTIC—IT'S BASIC TO FUTURE CONTENTMENT

My basic definition of future orientation emphasizes the need to be realistic, so the future seems almost as real as the present. Clearly, Erica's future orientation was not very well developed. As a result, she felt trapped, hopeless, and depressed.

The circumstances may vary with the individual, but the same pattern of unrealistic future orientation shows up in choosing life paths. Consider the following life scenarios:

■ A young divorcee decides to move to California to start over, though she's never been west of New Jersey.

■ A high school dropout joins the military for a secure job and a snappy uniform, despite the fact that he has never been able to follow orders without demonstrating anger and rebellion.

■ A department store sales clerk keeps registering for college courses "because everyone knows a college education is important," then dropping them halfway through the semester.

In each case, the goal is at odds with personal makeup, values, and/or abilities. Even if the goal were realistic and the person were to endure and achieve them, would it be worth the price? Not if the goal and personality weren't compatible.

Could I, a controlling personality and creative thinker, follow arbitrary orders in the army, for example? Maybe. But I'm sure I'd become progressively depressed by the fact that I had so little control over my life. Not only do the goals you establish need to be realistic, but they must be realistic *for you.*

If Erica had been honest with herself and accepted that she tired easily of people, had no tolerance for the need to do things that inconvenienced her, had no patience for baby talk and the world of a child, she would have approached the decision to become a mother differently. If she still opted for motherhood, she would have worked with insight and responsibility (perhaps through therapy or parenting courses) to make the psychological adjustments necessary for her to become a good mother, instead of the resentful, detached mother she was.

GLOBAL THINKING—OVERWHELMED BY THE IMPOSSIBLE

Sometimes a client comes in to my office and announces, "My life is a mess. I have to stop drinking, stop smoking, work hard, play more, lose weight, get a divorce. And I need to do all these things *now.*" Another client will come in and say, "I've got a number of things I need to work on, but the *first* thing I need to do is pay attention to my problems at work or else I might lose my job, and it's my livelihood. After that's settled, I need to address the problems I have with my oldest son. *Then* I'd like to tackle my weight problem."

See a difference in these two styles? The first reflects a shot-gun approach to dealing with problems, with no apparent sense of priority. The second is specific, reflecting a clear sense of realism in ordering the problems to be addressed.

Scientific research and my own clinical experience confirm a marked tendency in depressed individuals to think globally—they tend to see things in their entirety, at the expense of noticing important details that should figure in establishing priorities. In other words, a global thinker sees the forest but misses the trees.

Too much global thinking can encourage depression. Since every person's life surges ahead on many different fronts simul-taneously, it follows that multiple problems are nearly always present. The depressed person usually reacts to all the problems at once and feels so overwhelmed by them that he freezes up and either does nothing at all or gets distracted by irrelevancies. Such paralysis usually makes problems worse, which is why I continually emphasize the need to take charge and improve your ability to solve problems.

A global thinker knows what he wants in a general way, but he doesn't know how to get it. Do you say things to yourself like "I just want to be happy" or "I just don't want to be depressed anymore"? This is global thinking, and you can understand why things tend to go on being bad when you use this approach. Unless you have a specific series of steps to follow toward your goal, you are unlikely to achieve it.

Notice the global element in each of the following statements:

- "I want to make my life work."
- "I just don't want to fight with everyone all the time."
- "It seems like I am always depressed, no matter what I do."
- "People are so selfish. No one cares about me."

▪ "Life is so unfair. I don't deserve this."

▪ "All I want is a good relationship. Is that too much to ask?"

▪ "I want my job to go smoothly and not be such a hassle."

Thoughts like these could overwhelm anyone! Where do you start when there's no specific problem or specific person to deal with? Is anyone ever prepared to take on *life* and *everyone*?

THE STRUCTURE OF SUCCESS

I hear depressed people tell me they're aiming for financial security, but they freely admit they know nothing about financial matters. They tell me they want to write a book, but they don't know what the subject would be. They say they want to get a good job, but they don't know what kind of job or where to look for it. I hear scores of such global wants from my clients, none of whom have a specific plan for bringing their dreams to life.

I differ (some say radically) from many of my professional colleagues in my belief that there is a way to do damn near anything if you use the right approach. Now, that statement doesn't mean "Where there's a will, there's a way." Will is different from ability and strategy. Getting a good job *is* possible—people do it all the time. They also achieve financial security, marital satisfaction, good self-image, and everything else you might envy in others. You can do what they do and you can have what they have—*if* you can look beyond your heart's desire and develop a realistic plan that will get it for you.

Bear in mind, such accomplishments are not a matter of intelligence but of a *style* in thinking. They result from carefully planned, step-by-step moves toward an achievable goal. Take this book as an example. It took many months to research, write, rewrite, edit, design, and print the product you hold in your hand. It is the result of a goal met by following specific steps. In the same way, you must make an effort to learn about the steps

➡ **TAKE ACTION** ➡

Save Yourself Some Grief

If you know yourself, both your weaknesses and strengths, you can generally avoid potentially hazardous situations. The ability to do this is a vital preventive measure.

On a piece of paper, write out a list of the characteristics that best describe your personal makeup. Now go a step further and specify the behaviors, thoughts, and feelings that led you to that description. The essential element in this exercise is that you describe yourself *as you are*, not as you'd like to be. Use your list to identify situations that could be harmful to you. For example, Erica had a number of traits that should have deterred her from making the irreversible decision to become a mother.

Here is an example of how such a list might look.

Personal Characteristics	Indicators	Potentially Difficult Situations
Self-contained	I have difficulty in sharing myself with others.	Cocktail parties Public contact job
Short attention span	My mind wanders a lot and I'm generally inattentive.	Classroom lecture Detail-oriented job
Controlling personality	I always want things my way.	Children's field trip or birthday party Customer service job

that produce positive results for other people. Otherwise they will always seem smarter or better or luckier than you, and you'll always be frustrated in your wants and feel like a failure. If you don't know what so many others seem to know, it's time to ask why. You need someone to explain what you have to know.

PROBE FOR THE PROCESS

In my life, I have learned to deal with a variety of psychological problems, including depression. As a novice, I watched experienced professionals conduct impressive therapy sessions, and I seriously doubted that I could ever do such work. It was depressing to suspect that I might not succeed in my chosen profession. I found the formal academic training process limited in some ways. I would ask these truly gifted teachers why they approached a problem as they did in a demonstration. And often, too often for my taste, they responded simply that it just seemed like the right thing to do, that they followed an intuition.

The vagueness of such answers gave birth to my interest in learning how to structure procedures. Many successful people are unable to tell you how they do what they do so well. Some admit they themselves don't even know how they do it. That doesn't help much. But if you watch them, interview them, and study them, they almost always show a pattern, a sequence to what they do.

So sometimes you can learn specific sequences through explanations by an expert; other times it's up to you to figure it out. Some experts simply don't know how to explain the complex yet automatic process. (Think about trying to explain some of the intricate actions you perform daily. How do you tie your shoes? How do you decide what to wear? How do you drive? You are probably unaware of precisely how you accomplish these functions.)

Even if you do learn from others, you will most likely have to modify things for your unique needs and style. So you might not succeed, even when you do *exactly* what they do. For example, despite my very serious instructors, I had to find a way to use my sense of humor. In the process, I discovered it was okay to share laughter with a client. No one ever told me that in school.

As a psychologist, I see people at the best and the worst times in their lives. By keeping my eyes and ears open, I get to learn what does and doesn't work. In fact, this book is a direct

---

Living Skills We All Need   ➜ **LOOK DEEPER**

Some people have characteristics that make certain aspects of life easier for them than for the rest of us. We have to *learn* to do what comes naturally to them, but it's worth the effort.

Are you an organized person who knows how to establish priorities and when to address them, or are you someone who finds it difficult to prioritize and organize your concerns? What impact does your style have on your state of depression?

---

result of hearing about people exposed to all kinds of situations, including hurtful ones. And I ask questions about the consequences—who gets depressed and who doesn't? Many of the patterns I describe and urge you to learn are the same ones followed by people who seldom get depressed. Even when they do have a down period, it is brief and mild.

It's essential to remember that you don't have to know it all before you try to accomplish something. No one else does. Suppose you believe you know or should know how to do something (plan, work, relate, problem-solve). If you don't get the results you want when you do it one way—*do something else!* If you don't know what that something else is, *ask!* Don't let yourself sink into depression due to frustration and a sense of failure. Find a good therapist or consultant with a sound knowledge of whatever it is you want to do well. Learn to follow the steps that will help make your life what you want it to be, and depression will be a problem no more.

A NEW BEGINNING

Get started by establishing goals for each important area of your life and defining each goal in very specific terms. Identify a sequence of very specific steps leading to the goal. Seek out any factor that could alter your plans and have a contingency plan ready to go. Finally, establish a time line for achieving your goal.

You must find out when to pay attention to your feelings—and when to ignore them. The feeling of being overwhelmed, for example, is one you should ignore, since it can only paralyze you. Instead, focus on feelings of anticipation and enthusiasm for what needs to be done and on the priorities you set up for doing it.

How do you establish priorities? You can use the *time factor:* Suppose you must leave the house in half an hour to get to work on time. You have to shower, shave, find a clean shirt, polish your shoes, have breakfast, and read the paper. How do you make it all work out?

You *have* to be clean and dressed or you can't leave the house, so you take care of that first. Then, if you're the type who *needs* to eat in the morning, you plan on the minimum that will get you by. If you still have time, you polish your shoes (nice, but not essential) and then scan the paper during any minutes left before you're due to go out the door. Immediacy dictates your actions.

A second way to prioritize is according to *degree of importance:* The sink is overflowing, the phone is ringing, the baby is crawling toward the top of the cellar steps, and it's time to take the clothes out of the dryer. What's most important? The baby's safety, of course, then stemming the flood. If the phone's still ringing, answer it, and then take your clothes out of the dryer!

You can also prioritize according to *controllability,* deciding to invest your time and energy where you can actually make a difference, instead of wasting time on things you have no control over anyway. You have a free afternoon and your friend wants you to join her while she shops for drapes; you could use the time to plant some bulbs and trim the hedge. You know your friend won't accept your suggestions for colors or patterns and you'll end up feeling inadequate and frustrated—*and* you'll have

Visualize Your Possibilities

LOOK DEEPER

Remember the classic story *A Christmas Carol,* by Charles Dickens? In it, Ebenezer Scrooge is a miserable miser hated by all. And only when he is visited by the Ghost of Christmas *Future* does he realize the dire implications of continuing on his negative path. Scrooge changes his ways for the better when he envisions himself being remembered badly in the future.

Take some minutes of silence each day to close your eyes and quietly reflect on things you can do today to make your future brighter and happier. Build in yourself the expectations that can lead to better times ahead.

to squeeze the planting and trimming into your busy schedule later. What's your priority?

Each situation must be judged on its own merits, and appropriate priorities must be set. Good judgment about where and when to invest yourself is what it takes to minimize episodes of depression. In fact, that is why I wrote the first three chapters of this book as I did. I wanted to help you develop a sense of priorities about the depression experience and what you needed to learn about yours. Then you could manage your life better and consequently feel better. I also wanted you to understand there is no magic cure. But the right sequence of thoughts and behaviors can lead you to feel good about yourself and your life.

A FRESH ATTITUDE TOWARD THE FUTURE

Frustration, anger, and pain come from the feeling that things are hopeless, and they are the stuff depression is made of. I have focused your attention on the role played in depression by a

(continued on page 108)

Practice Planning

You probably don't realize how clever and capable you are. Every day you accomplish complicated actions, never realizing that you follow a definite sequence or plan to make each one work out. You must devise a similar sequence to get each of the things you desire in life, particularly if they seem to elude you.

Consider the simple activity of taking a shower. If you made a flow chart of all the steps involved, here's how it would go: First, you go into the bathroom, turn on the light, and open the shower door. You reach inside and turn on the water, testing it with your hand until you're comfortable with the temperature. Then you disrobe and step in . . .

Notice how many steps are involved with that simple act. What are the steps, then, for achieving something so complex as good relationships or personal satisfaction? You must master the ability to break such global goals into specific tangible steps. Probably everything you want to do is possible, but you must be armed with a realistic sequence that will bring it about. If you don't have one, then ask someone who does! Here is a sample of sequencing steps.

Goal: I want to go back to school and get a college degree so I can eventually have a better job.

Take the following steps to reach this goal:

1 Look up *Colleges* and *Universities* in the Yellow Pages.

2 Call or write to obtain a school catalog.

3 Identify their degree programs related to my career choice.

4 Review the course curricula in the catalogs.

5 Call to schedule meetings with school admissions counselors.

6 Review the school policies for admission, financial aid, and scheduling, the course structures and expectations, and the grading criteria to determine required effort.

7 Complete the application for admission.

8 Complete financial aid request forms (student loan applications).

9 Schedule classes.

10 Show up, look alert, and complete requirements for *every* class.

Now try your hand at planning the steps required to achieve a goal important to you.

KEY POINTS TO REMEMBER

- The ability to set positive, realistic goals and work toward them is fundamental to feeling good emotionally.

- It's important to be future oriented in a way that also permits a meaningful contact with your past and present.

- It is distorted thinking to see the future only as more of the same.

- A well-developed sense of future orientation opens the way to a higher rate of success in predicting the result of your actions. You can learn this sense for the future, and you get better at it with practice.

- You don't need to focus on the past to establish important and realistic goals for the future. In fact, looking to the past could be a mistake.

- Suicidal feelings are a distortion of reality because they spring from a hopeless assumption that things cannot get better. They can.

- Motivation is directly related to expectations of success.

- A sense of purpose is tied to goals for the future. With it, you can endure what would otherwise seem impossible to handle.

- Depression is often the result of letting yourself be trapped into a situation to accommodate others. You must make choices according to your own values and abilities.

- Global thinking—a lack of detailed plans, with no order of priorities—leads to feeling overwhelmed.

- Know your own preferences and limitations so you can avoid situations that would work against your nature. For example, if you want a lot of control over your career, don't join an organization that requires blind obedience.

- Global thinking prevents you from seeing the need for a realistic and specific sequence to attain your goals. If you know *what* you want but not *how* to get it, don't give up. You can learn what you need to know for success.

sense of the future and the influence of this sense on other aspects of your life. But you need a healthy balance in relating to the past and present, as well as the future, if you are to feel good and avoid depression.

Hopelessness springs from the lack of a realistic vision of what you can attain in life. You sink into your own feelings of despair at the very time you need to go outside of yourself and patiently learn to do what others seem to do so easily. If your path to success is blocked, don't come to a dead stop; try to discover a new path.

Neither you nor I can change your past. But tomorrow hasn't happened yet. What would you like to have happen? What about next week, next month, next year, and the years after that? The things you do now, today, lead to what happens tomorrow and all the tomorrows that follow. Use the skills you've learned to develop a positive and realistic future orientation. All the good things in your life will come from doing things both inside yourself and out in the world that make your life worthy in *your* eyes.

A positive future orientation is the starting point for developing everything else you need to defeat depression. Learn all you can learn, and you'll look back one day on how you turned your life around for the better. *Plan* on it.

Chapter 5

FIND OUT HOW OPTIMISM AND PESSIMISM DEFINE YOUR LIFE

There's an old joke about a young man who searched the world for an answer to the question, "What is the meaning of life?" In the temples of Nepal he learned of a guru living high in the Himalayas who could answer his question. So he arranged to make the difficult climb, braving freezing weather, avalanches, and rockslides. Physically exhausted, nearly delirious, he finally reached the cave of the guru. Trembling with anticipation, he asked the question, "Oh, great wise man, what is the meaning of life?" The guru paused, contemplated, and then answered, "Life is a bowl of cherries." The young man was incredulous, astonished. He took a step back and yelled, "That's it? That's it? Life is a bowl of cherries?" The guru said, "You mean it's not?"

This joke illustrates a point very well. Every human being on this planet defines the purpose of life in general, and the purpose of his own life in particular. Psychologists often use a famous device called the Rorschach inkblot test to help in assessing their patients' personal outlook. Subjects view a series of inkblots, one at a time, and describe what they see in each inkblot. Their interpretations range widely: various animals, people, and objects doing and experiencing all sorts of things. Each person sees the inkblot in terms of his own personal background and psychological makeup. The inkblots have no intrinsic meaning. They mean whatever people think they mean. Psychologists call this the *projection principle*: People faced with an ambiguous situation decide on its meaning based on what they know.

LIFE IS WHAT YOU MAKE IT

In a sense, we experience life as a Rorschach test. What could be more ambiguous than life itself? Both the Rorschach inkblot and life operate on the same principle: The meaning of things for each of us comes out of our own background, beliefs, and values. For example, of all the things I could have chosen for my career, I became a clinical psychologist. I see it as an important job that holds the potential for me to make a contribution to the well-being of people. But of course, many people have no interest in psychology and see no value in what I do. I've actually had people say to me, "Why be a psychologist? Don't you want a *real* job?" So, out of all the career possibilities, why did I choose psychology? Why did *you* decide to do what *you* do? Why do you think your job is important?

Life offers countless opportunities, and those we choose to pursue generally reflect our value system. In fact, we are the ones who give our lives meaning.

How Important Is Choosing?   → LOOK DEEPER

Many people think they chose neither their career nor their lifestyle. They feel they just fell into it. Do you think that it is a choice not to make a choice?

▶ **TAKE ACTION** ▶

Where Is Life Leading You?

Do you see a definite direction in the progress of your life? Will it take you where you want to go?

Review your lifestyle and write down the basic aspects of it (work, family, spiritual pursuits). Previously, you identified the core values you hold; with that in mind, do you see a theme emerging in the patterns of your life? How would you describe the meaning of your life?

Why is it important to have meaning and purpose in your life? Think about times when you had neither and felt adrift, and how that affected your mood and self-image. Now you have the opportunity to examine this process of making your life meaningful. You can evaluate whether the things that you once labeled important in your life actually were important. Have you assigned a purpose to your life? Is it to suffer and endure hardship? Seek a higher consciousness? Make money? Or simply to relax and have a good time and enjoy the ride?

WHAT'S IT ALL ABOUT, ANYWAY?

Making meaning out of life's ambiguity is what this chapter deals with. Our human nature leads us to make order out of chance or confusion. We have a need for things to make sense, so we can understand what's going on. Uncertainty creates an unpleasant, anxious internal state that must be resolved.

It's a basic human requirement that we evolve an explanation for every experience. If I asked you to explain why you chose the outfit you are wearing right now, you could probably do it. If you had to explain why you treat your friends as you do, you could probably tell me. If you were asked why you spend your money or time the way you do, you'd know what to say.

This raises a very important question that relates directly to your depression: How accurate or realistic are your explanations for the events of your life?

Suppose someone steers you wrong when you ask for information or advice concerning something you need to do. You have to explain to yourself why that happened. You might conclude that the person intentionally tried to deceive you; perhaps you'll guess that the person was himself poorly informed; maybe you'll decide it was up to you to double-check the information before acting on it. Regardless of what it is, you *will* reach a conclusion about why things happened the way they did.

As you go through each day, you continually explain things about yourself to yourself. You do the same about others and about the events around you. Each person develops a style for doing this. Your explanatory (or attributional) style plays a huge role in how you feel. Consider the earlier example in which someone gives you bad advice. If you conclude that it's your fault for not double-checking the information, you'll feel worse than you would if you concluded that your adviser was poorly informed. You can see how closely your feelings relate to how you explain the circumstances of your life.

LATE AGAIN—WHY?

Here is another example: Suppose you make plans for a friend to pick you up for dinner. It's 45 minutes after the time agreed upon, and your friend has not yet arrived. With each passing minute, you do a great deal of self-talk about your friend's no-show. As you'll see, the things you think about and say to yourself change your feelings, quite literally, from moment to moment.

At first you may simply think of your friend as being insensitive and irresponsible, and you find yourself feeling angry. Then, as time goes on, you may worry that something bad—an accident, an injury—prevented your friend from arriving on time.

You become concerned, even frightened. Maybe you start to feel that your friend cares little about you and that's why she's late, so you feel rejected, lonely, and even depressed. When your friend finally shows up, you feel relief first, then perhaps irritation surfaces, reflecting your feelings over the past 45 minutes of waiting and worrying.

That is a solid example of the relationship between your explanatory style and your internal mood. When you attribute irresponsibility to your friend, your reaction is anger; when you attribute the lateness to a possible catastrophe, you're worried and frightened; when you guess that maybe your friend just doesn't care about you, feelings of rejection, hurt, and depression well up.

"WHAT AM I TO THINK?"
THAT'S A RISKY QUESTION

Now you can see that ambiguous situations represent risk factors for you as a depressed person. Not everyone reacts to ambiguity in the same way. It is a learned reaction, so if your reaction sets you up to get hurt, it is time you learned to react differently.

LOOK DEEPER

Does Doubt Distress You?

Reflect on how you respond to ambiguity. When something is undefined for you, do you ask lots of questions in an effort to clear things up? Or do you let things remain clouded, passively assuming that answers will eventually emerge? People who do this show a tolerance for ambiguity. Assess your tolerance for ambiguity.

⟹ **TAKE ACTION** ⟹

Down with Overreaction!

Identify a recent event in your life that you reacted to in the extreme. How did you perceive the situation that generated such a reaction?

Identify the thought sequence that led to your reaction. For example, if you received a B on an examination and concluded "I'm a failure because I didn't get an A," or if you didn't get a promotion at work and concluded "I'm a loser," you'd be demonstrating extreme black-and-white thinking. Any time you respond to a situation with an all-or-none attitude, you reflect dichotomous thinking and a low tolerance of ambiguity.

Patterns for dealing with ambiguity relate to other patterns closely associated with depression. All are equally problematic in terms of the way a depressed person thinks and reacts. One such pattern is known as black-and-white (or dichotomous) thinking. Many people are so uncomfortable with uncertainty that they use their own thought process to clarify things by making them extreme, therefore unambiguous. Such a person sees a situation as black and white when almost anyone else would see it as gray. Obviously, that person isn't responding objectively to what is true or realistic.

QUESTIONS THAT HAVE NO WRONG ANSWER

I mentioned earlier that people do not like uncertainty, so they need to make sense out of their experiences. What happens when we apply this principle to situations where there is no sure meaning? Well, the person who is prone to extreme thinking will state his perceptions as if they were objective facts, even though they can't be demonstrated or proven in any way. For example, millions of people believe in astrology, even though there isn't one shred of objective evidence that the alignment of the stars affects your daily life. But if astrologers cannot prove the reality of their beliefs, no one can disprove it either. If I could disprove the validity of astrology, or if astrologers could prove its value, the issue would be settled. The same is true of countless similar questions.

If my client says, "The meaning of life is to suffer," how can I disprove it? It's a belief system, an obviously *arbitrary* belief system with no real evidence for or against it. The phenomenon of black-and-white thinking can lead people to react to arbitrary beliefs as though they are facts. In other individuals, that pattern is relatively harmless. But for you, a person prone to depression, it represents a hazard.

It is especially important that *you* learn to respond to objective evidence when it is available. For example, if you believe you are a person who doesn't deserve to be happy, you can phrase this belief as a question: What does a person have to do to deserve happiness? Obviously, there is no clear answer to that question. It's as ambiguous as "Is astrology real?" or "Is there a God?" There is no definitive answer. Any answer you generate is your reaction to a verbal inkblot. Your answer reflects what you believe or what your background leads you to believe, but it is not a definitive truth.

Part of learning to defeat depression soundly is learning to bypass questions that have no one unarguable answer. By now you should know why: Ambiguous situations put you at risk of projecting the most negative and self-hurtful interpretations. Consider the following scenarios and take note of the answers that occur to you.

Scenario 1: You leave a message on an answering machine requesting a return call; two or three days pass and the call is not returned. How do you interpret the lack of response to your message?

Scenario 2: You apply for a job that you want very much. Two weeks go by and you have not yet had an answer to your application. How do you interpret the delay?

Scenario 3: You meet a close friend for dinner, and through-out the evening he or she seems distant. How do you interpret your friend's demeanor?

WORST CASE RESPONSES

Think carefully about your reaction to these everyday situations. Is it positive, negative, or neutral? Now, on the basis of the principles described in this chapter, is it possible that you altered your responses from what they might have been other-wise? If you gave the response typical of a depressed person to Scenario 1 (the phone call not returned), you saw it as some sort of personal rejection or a lack of interest in you as a person. If your explanatory style is negative, you are unlikely to conclude

---

➡➡ **TAKE ACTION** ➡➡

Choose a Feel-Good Explanation

When friends don't show up for a date, when personnel directors don't say yes about the job, when people don't return a call left on their answering machine, some people see it as a signal of their unworthiness. "Why," they ask themselves, "would anyone bother with me anyway?" This kind of reaction is a strong invitation to depression. A healthier response is to presume a nonpersonal explanation—an accident, a better-qualified applicant, distraction due to business.

To make this point personally meaningful, write down ten situations that occurred recently and that resemble the structure of the scenarios just described—that is, events that have no clear explanation. For each of these scenarios from your own life, write out the explanations you generated and the feeling associated with each. What other explanations for the same events occur to you now that you have a little more emotional distance from those situations?

that the person you called was busy or had other priorities, or that the person was simply being lazy or irresponsible. Instead, you attribute the action as a fault of your own, not a statement about that person's experience.

In Scenario 2 (the unanswered application), you might have decided that two weeks without hearing anything was a bad omen for your job prospects. Again, if your style is negative, you probably saw this as evidence of a failure on your part, rather than evidence of inefficient methods in this company's hiring practices.

In Scenario 3 (a meeting lacking warmth), if your explanatory style is negative, you tend to interpret the distance as a rejection of you. You see it as a statement of your friend's disregard for you, rather than evidence of your friend's being preoccupied or immersed in some absorbing personal problem.

PLAN ON HOW YOU'LL HANDLE AMBIGUOUS SITUATIONS

So what's the point? Well, there are a couple of points here. First, you're learning that life serves up ambiguous situations on a steady basis, and you tend to interpret them according to your belief system and background. For a depressed person, these projections generally feed the negative thoughts and negative ruminations that add to the depression. Second, you're learning that your thoughts, and the interpretations (attributions) that you make, play a *very* large role in how you feel.

A preventive tip for you: Think ahead and try to discern any ambiguity in situations you encounter. Where will you get objective evidence to confirm a particular belief of yours? Does such objective evidence exist? Can you know in advance if there is no clear answer to your question, no objective information available anywhere?

For example, in Scenario 1, you have no objective information on why this person didn't call you back. You can come up

---

Take Advantage of Options

➤ **LOOK DEEPER**

Virtually every situation presents an option for action. Learn to look for the most comfortable way out of a problem. You'll see that you rarely have to settle for one that brings you pain.

As you learn to weigh your options, you become increasingly skilled at making deliberate choices about what will work best in a given situation. Can you anticipate how this ability will improve the quality of your life?

---

with all kinds of possibilities: The person is busy, doesn't like you, doesn't want to talk to you, misplaced your phone number, is out of town, and so forth. But in truth, only that person really knows why the call never came. Don't assume the worst. You can get objective information by asking that individual what happened.

In Scenario 2, only the potential employer can tell you what's going on. It's possible to ease your uncertainty by calling about the status of your job application, but deciding to call is not so simple. You have to consider whether it will work to your advantage (or disadvantage). It might make you feel better in the short run to find out what is going on; however, it is possible that your call might annoy the person doing the hiring. It's a judgment call. You might decide your rapport with the interviewer was good enough to permit the contact. The key point is, you learn to weigh your options, to think in terms of available possibilities and likely consequences for each option.

In Scenario 3, only your friend knows why he or she was distant. You can resolve the ambiguity by consulting your friend: "You seemed distant. Was something wrong?" Now, you face new decisions. Will your friend be annoyed at being questioned on this level? Or will your friend welcome the opportunity to explain that it was merely a problem at work or at home that took over that evening?

A SETUP FOR FRUSTRATION

It is absolutely vital to learn how to handle ambiguity if you want to prevent future depression. When you seek clarity in situations where clarity is impossible, you set yourself up for tremendous frustration. For example, many people are very strong in their belief that there is a God. Other people believe just as strongly that there is no God. In reality, when we look for objective evidence of the existence of God, there is none. No one can prove or disprove that God exists. So, if you ask, "Does God exist?" you'll be frustrated trying to find a clear and unambiguous answer.

Of course, that does not take away from the value of the role faith plays in life. Faith is a powerful aspect of experience that can bring many benefits. The point is that faith is different from objective truth. The same is true for other value-laden and personal-belief questions, such as: Is there an afterlife? How should I live my life? What's the ideal profession for me? Is there a perfect person for me to love? Is there one right way to do *anything?*

As someone prone to depression, you must learn to judge each situation on its own merits. No single rule applies in every case. Your task is to assess your strengths and weaknesses and

---

➡ TAKE ACTION ➡

Skip the Unanswerables

Write down the ambiguous questions you ask yourself that affect your mood. Do they include: "Am I a worthwhile person? Do I deserve to be happy? Is my life important? Will I ever be successful?" When you see how considering such questions paralyzes your self-improvement, you'll turn your attention toward action, rather than unproductive contemplation of the unanswerable.

regulate your actions to achieve a goal, not simply react to your feelings. You can find out how to recognize the situations that work in your favor and those that don't.

Suppose, for example, that you are the type who needs a great deal of approval. If you surround yourself with people who have difficulty expressing warm feelings, you're setting yourself up for emotional pain. To avoid risking such stress, you must tailor situations to meet your needs, values, and interests whenever possible. When you can't do that, at least realize it's not necessarily your fault when things don't go your way.

You must become skilled at avoiding conclusions that reflect only your own hurt and despair. Such negative views may fuel your depression if you accept false inferences as true. Here is the prescription: Get outside of your own interpretations so you can read them objectively. If you can't be objective due to a lack of solid information, you can at least pick the feel-good explanation.

Now you know attributional style is the way you choose to explain what happens in your life, both internally (feelings or thoughts) and externally (relationships to people and events). This gives you some new understanding about how your internal responses affect the way you handle each day's events.

TYPES OF ATTRIBUTIONS

We have specific ways to characterize each kind of attribution. These descriptions help you decide whether your attribution for a particular experience is appropriate.

Am I to Blame?
Internal/External Attributions

If you decide that whatever happens is due to you, that's an internal attribution. Consider the earlier scenario in which you meet a close friend for dinner. Your friend seems distant, so the internal attribution (explanation) might be "She is angry with me" or "He thinks I'm dull and really doesn't want to be with me." In essence, you blame yourself for the disappointing evening. That's how you choose to explain why such things happen as they do. Depressed thinking commonly leads a person to make internal attributions when, in fact, the situation is *not* internally based.

The opposite (external) type of attribution assumes that the situation is due to something outside yourself. In the scenario just discussed, you would conclude that something was not going right for your friend and he was distant because he was brooding about it—nothing to do with you.

Certainly, forming erroneous internal attributions—personalizing situations—is a common but distorted way of thinking among depressed individuals. Every time you personalize a negative event by putting yourself at the center of it, you are in the position of having to accept the blame for it. That doesn't feel good, and it leads to depression. The trick in managing attributional styles is to evaluate a situation correctly as internal (the first—but usually wrong—conclusion) or external (more often than not, the case).

Will It Always Be Like This?
Stable/Unstable Attributions

A person with a stable attributional style believes that life situations are unchangeable. The error lies in assuming that circumstances will remain the same when, in fact, they will not. So knowing how to tell when a situation really is or is not unchangeable (stable) is important. In contrast, the unstable attributional style considers most situations as potentially changeable. The healthier view is key to your level of motivation in therapy and your willingness to participate in your own recovery.

"I'm Just a Loser"
Global/Specific Attributions

When a person believes that any one experience impacts *everything* he does, that's a global attribution. A specific attributional style is particular to the situation at hand. Someone with a global style is more likely to say "I'm a loser" than "I'm not good at job interviews," a more specific appraisal. Part of learning to have a realistic and nondepressed attributional style is to be specific about things you experience. There's a world of difference between "I don't do very well on job interviews" and "I am a loser as a person."

Consider your own depression experience. If your view is "I'm depressed because I don't deserve to be happy," "I've always been depressed, I'll always be depressed," or "It affects everything I do," you can recognize your own *internal, stable,* and *global* attributional styles.

In fact, there is a very strong relationship between these attributional styles and depression. In treating depression, I continually have to teach my clients to be more external, unstable, and specific in their attributions about negative experiences. In other words, I want the person to realize that he isn't necessarily the one to blame, it doesn't necessarily affect all that he does, and it won't necessarily always be this way.

Sometimes the situation is the problem; it's going to change, and it's only that one specific type of situation that's a problem. Discovering how to tell objectively whether the attribution should be internal or external, stable or unstable, or global or specific is basic to recovering from depression and preventing future episodes. This chapter has already demonstrated how you project negativity into ambiguous situations, how you tend to think in extreme forms that make your perceptions lean toward black and white rather than gray, and how that kind of thinking can lead you to respond to situations incorrectly. Of course, if you handle situations ineffectively and conclude that you're no good or unworthy, that global attribution reinforces depression.

IS YOUR GLASS HALF-EMPTY OR HALF-FULL?

You can see how your general outlook on life is related to your explanatory or attributional style. If you consistently view situations in a negative way and predict an unpleasant future, you're a pessimist. If you view things positively, predict good things in the future, and choose the plus side in ambiguous situations, you're an optimist. Obviously, optimists feel better than pessimists. Think of the glass that can be seen as half-full or half-empty. The amount of liquid in the glass is constant; it's the attitude that changes.

We know that the person who thinks of life as half-full feels better than the one who sees it as half-empty. But which interpretation is right? Who knows? Those who have considered this question have concluded that reality is whatever you think it is. For those who believe that astrology is real, it's real; for the person who believes God exists, God exists; for those who believe dreams have meaning, dreams have meaning. Your beliefs dictate your actions and your attitudes. Since attitude plays such a large role in how you feel, you must monitor your beliefs, evaluating each one to see if it works for you or against you.

Test Your Beliefs

→ **LOOK DEEPER**

The same deep belief that can provide true comfort for one person can cause real misery for another. Such a belief might be at the root of your depression. Try to take an objective look at the principles you hold dear and see what they're doing to or for you.

How do you feel about being told that you will always have to monitor your beliefs? Can you see how it will empower you if you step outside of a personal conviction to consider its relative usefulness, rather than remain unable to question its role in your life?

Finding out how to examine your own explanations for events will play a significant role in how you feel about yourself, your life, and your future. Your attributional style affects not only your depression but also your level of productivity and your physical health. Attributional style impacts mood, mood impacts physiology and the course of action that you take.

JOHN DEMANDS THE IMPOSSIBLE OF HIMSELF

Let's consider the relationship between attributional style and level of productivity by looking at John, a client of mine.

John is a salesman, selling plumbing parts to building contractors. Of course, his success depends on selling as many plumbing parts as possible to all the contractors who build residential, commercial, or industrial buildings. John would like to monopolize the market, with all the contractors using only plumbing parts produced by his company. But John has competition. Other manufacturers also want to sell their plumbing products to the contractors. John is confident of the quality of his company's products, but he recognizes that competing companies can sell the same parts, although of lesser quality, cheaper. John is so sure that his parts are superior that he charges himself with making every call result in an order for parts. John's ambition is noble, but misguided.

John came to see me, feeling very discouraged about his work. He would awaken in the early morning, anxious about whether he would make enough sales to earn the commissions that he lives on. He was irritable at home and withdrawn from his wife and children—in short, presenting the classic signs of depression.

I asked John, "What factors influence whether a contractor purchases your parts?" John's immediate answer was "My ability as a salesman." "Is that the only factor that determines whether or not you make a sale?" I asked. His automatic answer was "Yes."

From that exchange alone, you should see why John is so anxious and depressed. Realistically, what salesman of *any* product sells all of his customers on every visit? What is the effect of John's taking all the responsibility for a successful sale on himself? Isn't it interesting that John sees no factors, other than personal (internal) ones, dictating his success as a salesperson?

I asked John if other factors also influence the sale. He was taken aback. "Like what?" he asked. I said, "Isn't it true that other people sell a similar product at a cheaper price?" He said, "Yes," and then added defensively, "But that product is not as good." I asked, "Aren't there some buyers who only consider price, care little about the quality of the product, and just want an adequate, inexpensive part?" John reluctantly agreed. "Yes, some people consider price alone."

I also asked, "Isn't it true that some of the people you call on may have had an extremely bad morning and may be concerned about existing debts at the time when you are asking them to create another expense?" Hesitantly, John agreed. I said, "Isn't it true that some people will not be responsive to you simply because they have already made a deal somewhere else, but they don't tell you to avoid getting into a discussion over the two products?" Hesitantly, John agreed. I continued identifying many factors that might influence a sale that had nothing to do with John's salesmanship skills.

It was as though I turned on a light bulb in John's head. All of a sudden it was obvious to him that no salesman could expect to sell to everybody. Instead of blaming himself, he saw that there were many, many *external* reasons for why he would not be 100 percent successful. John was actually cheered by the recognition that in fact, he was successful on 80 percent of his sales calls. His new perspective about his work permitted him to feel good for how much he did accomplish as a salesman for this company.

IT'S USELESS, SO WHY TRY?

John's case illustrates how a person's attributional style affects mood and outlook and productivity. John had begun to avoid making calls and meeting new contractors. He attributed this to the fear of failure and rejection when making a sale was his only criterion for success.

The relationship between attributional style and level of achievement is being examined in work and school environments. For example, the reasons a child with great intelligence and academic ability produces only Cs and Ds may have little to do with the teacher, the classroom, or the other students but may owe much to the child's attributional style. The child may see no reason to learn. If there's no future orientation about the worth of an education in his life, the motivation to learn will be marginal, and grades will reflect that.

Similarly, if a worker doesn't see any opportunity for professional or personal gain (no promotion, no raise, no special recognition), why should he bother to perform? As you saw in the last chapter, motivation is strongly tied to a person's sense of a positive future outcome.

So one way to think about your own level of motivation is to think in terms of your attributional style. If you make internal ("It's my fault"), stable ("It won't change"), and global ("It affects everything") attributions, your output and level of achievement will suffer, simply because your motivation has been sapped. That is a statement about your level of motivation, *not* your level of ability.

Attributional style also plays a role in your general level of health and well-being. It is well known that depressed individuals tend to have a higher rate of physical illness than others. In young people, illness generally takes very simple forms—occasional headache, backache, flu symptoms, fatigue, and so forth. Around age 45, something seems to happen that signals a more serious decline in physical health if the depression isn't adequately addressed. No one seems to know why, but supportive data is being gathered.

Your level of depression affects your immune system in ways that are now being studied in a relatively new field called *psychoneuroimmunology*. The relationship between mood states and diseases such as cancer is being examined, along with a relationship between outlook (relative degree of optimism or pessimism) and general health. Depression seems to weaken the immune system, the body's natural defense against disease, so disease can get a foothold in your body. Defeating your depression will promote better physical health to go along with your improved emotional well-being.

As the fatigue associated with depression dwindles away, you should take deliberate steps to improve your health. Whether you get into an exercise program or physical training (walking, swimming, karate, fencing, tennis), using your body in ways to make it strong and harmonious with your feelings is essential to long-term recovery from any illness or impairment, including depression. The fact that your mood plays a strong role in your body's natural defense system is an important piece of preventive information. So if you learn to avoid all the pitfalls associated with depression, you're bound to feel better physically as well.

GUARD AGAINST THE PERILS OF PESSIMISM

Your own level of optimism and pessimism reflects the way you think about your life and the world around you. It's important for you to avoid the hazards I described in this chapter: dealing with ambiguous situations as if they were not, thinking in black-and-white terms, personalizing things that aren't personal, viewing things as unchangeable, and responding globally instead of dealing with specifics. You continually run the risk of reinforcing attributions that maintain pessimism and, consequently, bad humor, low productivity, and poor health.

This chapter orients you to the nature of your own attributional style. You are able to develop a tolerance for ambiguity when that's necessary, identify sources of clarity when they exist, learn the arbitrary nature of the way you interpret experience (which can serve to fuel the despair and negativity of depression), and avoid getting attached to these interpretations as real or true.

You must learn to judge each situation on its own merits, effectively search out and make use of facts when they exist, and

KEY POINTS TO REMEMBER

- Human nature demands that we develop meaning and understanding in interpreting life's events.
- People in ambiguous situations (meaning there is no one clear interpretation) project meaning according to their background and their frame of reference.
- Since life is ambiguous, the understandings and explanations that you have for the events of life play a huge role in how you feel.
- When you face situations that are ambiguous, you risk depression if you interpret them negatively.
- People prone to depression must learn to respond to available, objective evidence.
- By recognizing ambiguity in situations, you can learn to weigh your options and the likely consequences of each option.
- Each situation in life must be judged on its own merits.
- Learn how to regulate your actions to achieve the result you want, and *don't act* simply according to how you feel.
- Explanations or attributions for an experience can be described as internal or external, stable or unstable, or global or specific. Depressed people most frequently make attributions that are internal, stable, and global for negative experiences.

invest less of yourself in explaining good *or* bad—which can't be proved anyway. You can control your degree of emotional involvement with experiences, protecting yourself from investing too heavily in a viewpoint that is arbitrary and hurtful and that may eventually prove false.

In essence, I strongly encourage you to increase your response to what's out there in the world around you rather than to what is in your head, especially when your thoughts generate pain and depression. The things you want for yourself—peace of mind, the comfort of a well-run, well-balanced life—are good and reasonable things to want. What you're learning, I hope, is that there are ways to get what you want, especially if you don't get bogged down with arbitrary and hurtful explanations that hold you in depression's grip.

Chapter 6

LEARN THE LIMITS
OF YOUR CONTROL

Consider the state of the world today, with all its political hot spots. Threats of widespread violence exist in all too many places. If we search out the reason for centuries of human aggression, we find that people fight and die for beliefs that seem, objectively speaking, arbitrary and subjective. Conflicts ranging from international to personal often spring from an intolerance of others who believe or act differently from the aggressor's conception of what is right. Beneath the surface, aggression is a need to control not only the beliefs and spiritual connections of others but also their behaviors and the way they live their lives.

Let's consider this need to control life situations and control other people—and how your ability to manage control relates to your experience of depression. I noted before that your perspectives about control are closely related to depression. Looking more closely at the way you deal with control will help you understand it better. I cannot think of one depressed person I ever treated who was entirely clear about the issue of control. Distorted ideas about what you can and cannot control lead you to respond inappropriately to life situations, and that can escalate to depression when things deteriorate.

Understand the Meaning of Control

I repeatedly use the term *control* when I discuss depression. What do you think I mean by the word? What is *your* definition of control? What does it mean when someone is described as a controlling person?

When I talk about control, I refer to the power or capacity for influence you have in any given situation. You are learning to react to each situation and that situation's dynamics rather than to your feelings or expectations. So, if you consistently underestimate or overestimate your power, you risk misreading situations that can then hurt you and trigger episodes of depression. I hope the ideas and techniques in this chapter will help you develop a clear concept of the issue of control. Once you have it, you can anticipate when it is to your advantage to move into a situation and make things happen. You also know when it is better to let a situation sail by, because no amount of effort on your part will make a difference.

Your Role: Controller or Controlled?

Are you a controlling person or one who is more likely to be controlled by others? How do you know? When has your pattern for dealing with control worked *for* you? When has it worked *against* you? Think of specific examples. Try to work out a safe strategy regarding control.

SOCIETY'S RULES SET UP THE NEED FOR CONTROL

Every society and component of society, including the family, has rules that all members agree to obey. That results in stability as well as security. For example, it is to your advantage that all drivers agree to follow traffic rules; you certainly don't want to meet a car driving south in your lane as you drive north!

Of course, it's necessary to have clear and explicit rules to regulate our behavior. But it's also true that rules must be bent or broken if progressive change is to occur. As an example, consider feminism as a movement that shaped our current perceptions of women's roles. Twenty-five years ago, a woman who wanted to work outside of the home felt she had to justify her position to friends and relatives. Today most women work outside of the home, and the scenario is reversed. *Now* women who "only" want to stay at home and raise a family feel a need to explain why they're not out there competing in the professional world.

This huge social change came about in a very short period of time. Many of us welcome such changes and have little difficulty letting go of past traditions in favor of what seems to be progress. However, such changes produce a great deal of anxiety

---

LOOK DEEPER

Explore the Need to Break Rules

Have you ever had to break rules to accomplish worthwhile things in your life? If so, how did you know it was necessary to do what you did? How did you handle the reactions of others? Would you do it again if you were in the same situation?

and discomfort for others, because they lose a sense of security about what is customary and appropriate behavior.

Those who violate social custom frequently face disapproval and rejection. Some may never know that their rule-breaking behavior led to progressive personal or social change. Some discover that they broke rules blindly, fighting just to fight, with little or nothing of importance to gain.

FAMILY CONTROL STARTS AT THE CRADLE

Whether you realize it or not, you have been molded by the expectations of others. And who are those others? For most of us, the most powerful of all the socialization agents is our family. The issue of control is most prominent in the earliest years of your life. As a helpless infant and then as a young child, your family controls your behavior almost entirely. The family dresses you, feeds you, responds to your cry, talks to you, educates you, and teaches you to view the world as they do. So, as you are required to obey the demands of your parents, you are learning to develop control over yourself. You learn what you may not say or do, where you may not go, and which experiences you may not have.

Paradoxically, the more you learn to control yourself to suppress characteristics others call undesirable, the more you are controlled by the people who come up with these judgments. Unfortunately, these labels lead you to see those characteristics in the same negative ways. To be controlled by others, at least to some extent, is inevitable; no one entirely escapes the influence of others.

Fortunately, some parents are sensitive to the issue of control. They take deliberate steps to foster a healthy sense of personal control and independence in their children as early as possible. Some mothers let children of an appropriate age choose the clothes they wear to school; other mothers lay out the child's clothes the night before. The latter practice effectively excludes the child from the decision process and unintentionally establishes that she has no control, even when it comes to something as simple as what she wears.

Consider your own family. Did your parents encourage you to take relatively safe risks, such as exploring your immediate environment? Or were you kept within close reach because of the potential for danger everywhere? Were you encouraged to make your own choices about what to wear, what games to play, what friends to have? Or were these imposed upon you?

Your sense of control results from repeated interactions that reinforce the perception that you either *make* things happen or that things happen *to* you. A distorted view of the issue of control can lead to misjudgments that continually chip away at your self-esteem and make you feel incompetent.

⇒ **TAKE ACTION** ⇒

How Did You Get This Way?

Why do you flinch when acquaintances use rough language? How is it that you always count your change at the market? What's your reason for ignoring pleas from organized charities? A good way to learn where many of your ideas about life came from is to think about the rules of your family.

Write out a statement of rules you grew up with, spoken or unspoken directions on the *right* way to live. For example, what were the rules about expressing your feelings, being ambitious, handling money, talking about sex, solving personal problems, and other elements of growing up? What impact did each rule you listed have on your life? Are these rules you should continue to follow, or should you bend or break some of them so you can feel better?

THE NEED FOR CONTROL MEANS YOU'RE HUMAN

Why do we need explanations and an understanding of the things that go on in the world around us? This need is an intense motivating force for gathering information, sorting through it, and attempting to use that data to make things happen. The need to understand is just one manifestation of the need we have to control our environment.

When we can explain things, we feel better. We can believe we have some insight into the relationship between cause and effect, even if we can't prove the explanation we develop. Certainly, organized religion is a strong example of this phenomenon. The world has scores of religions, each held sacred by its followers. Each one is certain that its own views are inherently correct. And each one is dedicated to the belief that since it is undoubtedly the *correct* religion, the other religions must be wrong. This encourages devaluing the beliefs of others and justifies treating them without deference.

The same phenomenon occurs in clinical psychology. Scores of psychological theories exist, each as unprovable as the next. Each theory has its followers, who believe their views are inherently correct and any dissimilar views are wrong. Professional colleagues who believe as I do will find this book useful and may recommend it to their depressed clients. Those who believe otherwise will find the ideas here too different and will discount the book's value on that basis.

Many people are so psychologically fragile that they need to maintain a rigid belief system that satisfies their need to understand. It is the only way they can feel a sense of personal control. Such people are highly volatile, exploding if they sense their beliefs are being questioned or discounted. This apparent strong reaction actually reflects uncertainty and shows how important it is for them to hang on tightly to a subjective belief. A live-and-let-live attitude would be a considerably more sophisticated way of going through life.

WORKING WITHOUT A NET

This need to control surfaces in many ways. Among the most prominent is behaving in a way that creates an illusion of control. Think of the old saying "There are no atheists in foxholes." Try to interpret that saying in terms of the issue of control. In essence, it suggests that someone in a foxhole during a military battle, with bombs exploding all around and bullets whizzing overhead, does not and cannot feel in control of his life. He knows *he's* not in control, but he certainly hopes *someone* (or something) is! Who could that someone be but God?

▶ TAKE ACTION ▶

Should You Take the Bows and the Blame?

Are you always responsible when things don't work out as you want them to? If you analyze such situations, you will discover that many personal disappointments were due to external forces, utterly beyond your control. Learn when to excuse yourself if an effort proves unsuccessful.

For each of the following situations, list the variables that influence the desired result, and estimate the percent control you have over getting what you want. (100 percent equals total control; 0 percent equals no control.)

▸ You apply for a job you really want.

▸ You intend to ask someone you're interested in for a date.

▸ You buy a present for a relative in the hope that he will be thrilled with it.

▸ You buy some new clothes to impress someone.

▸ You negotiate with a car salesperson, trying to buy a new car at the best possible price.

Now do the same exercise with five important situations in your own life.

Many soldiers in the heat of battle have a spiritual awakening that leads them to pray earnestly for safe deliverance from the battlefield. They make promises to reform their behavior, be more charitable, and live a saintly future, if only they are allowed to survive the battle. The spiritual awakening and the bargaining with God are obvious attempts to exercise some control in a situation that is otherwise entirely out of control. The well-known religious conversion that often takes place among prisoners on Death Row is another example of this phenomenon.

There's nothing wrong or pathological in seeking control over what happens in your life; this need for control is absolutely basic. The question is how *you* recognize and assert patterns of control. Wanting more control over your life is perfectly fine, but problems arise when your wants and the situation at hand don't match. When I see a client who has a so-called control issue, I'm not concerned about his desire to control his life. Anyone who is effective faces control issues; the wisdom lies in knowing when to respond to them and when not to.

DISTORTED IDEAS ABOUT CONTROL

The errors in judgment people make about the issue of control fall into two categories: distortions that create an illusion of helplessness, and distortions that create an illusion of control. In the illusion-of-helplessness situation, you see yourself as having no control when you do have control. In the illusion-of-control situation, you have an inflated sense of control and think you can control circumstances that you really can't control. Let's look at each category in greater depth.

Make a Move, Marie!
The Illusion of Helplessness

Have you noticed the tendency in depressed individuals to let hurtful situations go on hurting them? In effect, they act as though they are utterly helpless to improve things when, in fact, they are not helpless at all.

I remember treating a young woman named Marie for depression. She felt her depression originated at her job, and now it had begun to interfere with all aspects of her life. She felt hopeless all the time and had no motivation to do anything.

Marie told me she played a key role in the office where she worked but that her job had become increasingly intolerable. She took full responsibility for her attitude and blamed herself for feeling so negative about her job. She told of how her boss frequently announced, at the last minute, that she must work overtime, with no concern about disrupting her plans. Marie said she couldn't be promoted because hers was the only position in the small business. Further, she was already at the top of her pay scale and was ineligible for any raises other than small cost-of-living increases.

All in all, Marie described a dead-end job, and trying to adjust to it only increased her level of depression. Of course, Marie had no support from others at work, and because her job monopolized so much of her time and attention, she had no real friends outside the job to lend emotional support either.

My straightforward advice to Marie was to find another job. That possibility had never occurred to her, obvious as it might seem to anyone else. Why did Marie respond so helplessly to a situation over which she had some control? Marie didn't have to stay in that hurtful situation; she could find (or develop) a new and better job for herself. Any therapist who has worked with depressed clients has seen individuals like Marie who neglect to take what seem to be obvious steps to help themselves. How does this happen?

In the first chapter I described Martin Seligman's learned helplessness theory. Seligman was perplexed at how most depressed people accepted negative and painful experiences so passively. His research on this problem provided many valuable insights into depression, and I want to share them with you. Any beliefs you may have about being helpless yourself will be challenged as you read on.

━━━━━━━━━━━━━▶ **TAKE ACTION** ▶━━━

Evaluate the True State of Your Helplessness

Do you feel helpless to change certain unhappy situations you face? Why do you feel that way? Can you think of what someone else might do differently to handle the situation better? Generate some options for yourself; if necessary, poll others about what they would do, so you can get other perspectives.

Seligman exposed research subjects to painful events (loud or obnoxious noise, for instance) that were inescapable and beyond their control. At first they tried to escape this negative situation, but they couldn't do so immediately. Eventually they gave up trying and they immediately developed obvious symptoms of depression—apathy, withdrawal, sleep disturbance, agitation, and so forth. In itself, this showed how painful circumstances can cause depression in some people.

Not all the research subjects became depressed, however. Here the factor of stable attributional style (the belief that things won't ever change) worked against those who became depressed. Seeing things as unstable—that is, changeable—can work to prevent helplessness.

A further insight into learned helplessness came in the next phase of the experiment. Those who had been exposed to the uncontrollable negative events, who felt helpless and became depressed, were placed in a situation where they could easily escape these events. Even though this time there was some *possibility* of escape, the subjects did nothing to help themselves. Apparently, because they learned before that there was nothing they could do when they were being hurt, they didn't even try in the new situation! Seligman termed this phenomenon learned helplessness.

The implications of this research for understanding depression are far-reaching. Consider what happens to someone who is frequently punished for no apparent reason. For example, suppose you grew up in a household where you got punished one day for doing something, and the same behavior was ignored the day after. You might easily conclude that life is unpredictable, uncontrollable, and that the only thing to do would be to accept whatever miserable fate comes your way.

An important postscript to Seligman's experiments concerns treatment. Once the research subjects concluded that they were helpless and had to passively accept pain, attempts to teach them that they were now in control, able to exert influence over their own experience—even with lessons on how to prevent or escape from punishment—were met with indifference. They showed no ability to absorb the new learning. It took many, many trials before the subjects could overcome the limitations of their previous learnings of helplessness, so they could recognize opportunities for helping themselves. However, you can learn quickly from this research that helplessness is a frame of mind, *not* a reality.

It is fundamental to your recovery from depression that you integrate the realization deep down that it is a distorted viewpoint to assume you are generally helpless in life. In fact, no one's life is totally beyond his own influence. Even when you can't change circumstances, you *can* change your reaction to those circumstances. The feeling of helplessness, seeing yourself as out of control, is liable to trigger depression.

When you do feel that way, you must automatically make a rapid assessment of whether the circumstances actually are beyond your control. Depressed individuals, because of their distorted thinking, tend to see themselves as helpless when they're not. You might blame yourself for being ineffective or incompetent when, in fact, *no one* could have done anything better. As you will see in chapter 8, depressed people tend to take things personally that are not personal at all.

► LOOK DEEPER

Are You the Critic Who Puts You Down?

It's easy to understand that many people learn to give up without even trying to help themselves after being exposed to hurtful experiences beyond their control (childhood sexual abuse, battering, emotional abuse, or isolation). Such experiences are external and no fault of the individual, but what happens when such experiences are *internal?* For example, what if the critic who puts you down for everything you do lives in your head? You cannot eliminate him since he is a part of you, but you can learn to limit his influence. Contradict him with some positive statements about yourself. Consider how his impact would change if you thought of him as the school fool.

I Can Make Anything Go My Way!
The Illusion of Control

The previous section focused on the perception that you have no control when you actually do; this section focuses on the reverse, where you think you have control when you really do not. This is the illusion of control. It leads people to try things beyond their abilities, and then they suffer depression when those things don't go well.

Let me remind you of the statistic, mentioned early in this book, showing that Baby Boomers are especially vulnerable to depression. What is it about this group that might account for such a phenomenon? There is no one single factor; there are many. However, I firmly believe that one major reason Boomers are so depressed is their illusion of control. Most Boomers grew up thinking they could have anything—advanced education, a high-paying job, world travel, a family—and succeed in every endeavor. In fact, Baby Boomers *did* succeed professionally and financially much more quickly than their parents did. However, the downside is that too often they succeeded at the sacrifice of a balanced perspective on life and high-quality marital and family relationships, as the divorce statistics clearly illustrate.

It's a trap to believe you can get anything you want if you just approach it properly, and the high rate of depression emphasizes that fact. In some ways, success is actually a liability. When you are bright and successful, you do tend to believe you can do anything. If only that were true! Its widespread appeal as a basic belief comes from the comfort such thinking provides. It even spreads to health, where the view holds that if you think of the right things at the right level of intensity, you can heal yourself of cancer and other life-threatening illnesses. I think it is dangerous to promote such illusions of control with such sparse supportive evidence.

Ironically, I travel all over the world teaching workshops on clinical hypnosis, in which the mind/body connection is utilized intensively. I need no convincing that the mind can influence the body in positive ways. But I do need *lots* of convincing that the mechanism is reliable enough to use in treatment—"Visualize this and you will be cured." Desperate patients who *don't* get

---

Words to Live By?   ▶ **LOOK DEEPER**

Even the most time-honored mottoes don't always apply to everybody. Remember that we are individuals and we don't have a one-size-fits-all psyche. Before you saddle yourself with unnecessary or counterproductive psychological obligations, try to analyze the potential result.

What do you think of the saying "Where there's a will, there's a way"? Every child has heard it a hundred times. It sounds like a fine motivator, but is it right for you? Try to imagine how that attitude might place you at risk for depression.

Is Control Possible for You?   **LOOK DEEPER**

This book holds that you can control your depression. Does that idea encourage the illusion of control? Or is it possible that some important things really can be controlled if the right approach is used? You must practice every "Take Action" exercise and consider each "Look Deeper" suggestion. They will help you to know if you are winning the struggle against the illusion of helplessness or the illusion of control.

---

better get even more depressed when they are told they "probably don't really want to live." The illusion of control is a complex phenomenon, and it must be carefully considered.

The Baby Boomers were socialized in a unique era. Technological advances skyrocketed, social change was fast-paced, massive amounts of information became readily accessible in many forms, and greater economic security permitted a marked increase in consumer purchases. In general, people in this age group got what they wanted almost on demand. What does such instant gratification do to mental health? What is the effect on later expectations and experiences? Of course, I can't say conclusively that this high expectation of success is the main cause for the high incidence of depression in this group. However, it follows that a person who has been led to believe that motivation produces desired results ("Where there's a will . . .") is unprepared to deal with the reality if things don't happen that way.

The expectation of obtaining something simply because you want it has led many Boomers to think they can have it all. Depression may come to such individuals as a result of having to face the fact that no one can have it all.

Every choice you make precludes other choices. For example, striving to build a successful career means less time and emotional availability for building deep and satisfying relationships.

Choosing to have children precludes the ability to travel spontaneously while school is in session. Making achievement the object of intense focus precludes developing a sense of comfort with just *being* and not achieving at all.

Life involves many difficult choices, each with its own profound implications. The illusion that you can control all aspects of your life, with only desirable, happy consequences from the choices you make, is terribly unrealistic. Having it all is not the only way the illusion of control comes through. Anytime you try to make something happen that is not *directly* and *entirely* within your control, you may be laboring under an *illusion* of control.

The illusion is born of an idealistic desire we all have to make the world as we want it to be. It's important to want things to happen a certain way (we need to have positive goals), but our goals must be realistic. People who tend toward the illusion of control risk depression when they attempt to achieve unrealistic goals. A vital skill for controlling depression is the ability to identify clearly and consistently what is and is not within your control.

Caroline, a Woman Denied Control

I can think of many clients who attempted to make situations or people meet their needs and wants and entered a deep depression when the things they wanted most eluded them. The case of a middle-aged, deeply depressed woman named Caroline comes to mind. Her beloved college-age son was growing increasingly hostile toward her. In fact, the relationship was so strained she thought it was in danger of breaking. He attended an out-of-state college, and though he used to come home for frequent visits, now he came home very infrequently and seemed to have a chip on his shoulder.

Caroline had always done her best for her son, giving him everything she could, including piano lessons, extracurricular courses in foreign languages, and other academic advantages she considered important. At first, when he came home from college on weekends, she made a point of taking him to art galleries, museums, operas, music recitals, and any other cultural event she could find. From her narrative, I could see that Caroline exerted enormous pressure on her son to have him appreciate the things she deemed necessary to success in life. He had complied until he went away to school.

Now, as a maturing young adult, he felt capable of deciding for himself what was important in terms of his own energy and interests. Instead of acknowledging her son's increased maturity, Caroline increased the pressure on him to accept her values. She often told him angrily that if he were truly grown up, he would recognize the importance of what she was sharing with him.

Caroline is an example of one person's attempt to impose her idea of right, valuable, and necessary on another. She was driving her son away by not recognizing his right to choose for himself.

You *cannot* control another person. You may try to manipulate and exert pressure on that person to get the response you want, but eventually he will rebel. That one person would even attempt to control another signals an illusion of control. If you want to make someone in your life feel a certain way, respond a certain way, or reflect your values, don't fall into the trap of believing you can make this person do as you wish if you do everything right, for that is an illusion of control. You can't make anything go your way when the outcome is controlled by someone else.

Examples of failure in this pattern are abundant. Think of the women who say things like "If I could lose 20 pounds my husband wouldn't cheat on me" or "If only I were less demanding, he would stop drinking." Not true! The partner must make independent choices regarding fidelity or sobriety. If a woman believes her husband's choices are due to her weight or the level of her demands, she risks feeling very depressed when she does everything right and he continues his affair or goes on a drinking binge. You can care about others, even help support others, but you cannot control them.

You cannot *make* a person like you. You can do things you

━━━━━━━━━━━━━━━━━━━━━━━━━━➡ **TAKE ACTION** ➡━━

Test Your Powers of Persuasion

Here is an exercise in control. It will help you to see how difficult it is to *make* people change just because you say they should.

Pick a subject you know each of your friends cares about passionately. Attempt to convince each one to change his or her viewpoint. (Use only issues you are indifferent to, so you don't get emotionally involved in the discussion.) Can you change your friends' attitudes? How would you feel about their responses if you really wanted them to believe what you say?

think will make him like you, but that's based on *your* ideas of what *you* would like if *you* were that person. Self-centered (egocentric) thinking is common among depressed people. They literally think, "I wouldn't do that to anyone, so no one would do that to me." They are unguarded, and they risk total devastation by discovering that the other person *would* do that!

I assure you, other people do *not* value what you value, other people do *not* see things as you see things, and other people have different rules than yours for playing the game of life. If you want to be truly effective, learn about what other people value on their own, without prodding from you.

If someone's values differ from yours, you can either accept that fact and maintain a relationship while avoiding conflict over that issue or, if conflict is unavoidable, respect the person's choices and, if necessary, go your own way. Trying to control (change) that person's views is an effort that is likely to fail. The more emotion you invest in the doomed effort, the more you will judge yourself a failure and be depressed.

You cannot make your child value a clean room. You cannot make your insensitive partner sensitive. You cannot make someone think you are interesting and attractive. You can only be who you are. Regardless of who you are, some people will like you,

---

▶ **TAKE ACTION** ▶

Learn the Price of Universal Approval

The fear of rejection and the aversion to conflict are the usual reasons that some individuals try so hard to be liked. But how far can you go? How far would *you* go?

Get a concrete idea of your own willingness to give up control. Choose harmless environments and spend a day or two approval-seeking in the extreme. Ask permission for *everything* you do. "Do you mind if I go to the bathroom? Is it all right if I get some water? Is it okay if I order the fish?" How does this kind of pattern make you feel about the need to set your own standards?

---

some won't, and most will be indifferent. You can stand on a street corner passing out $100 bills, and some will be very happy with you, but others will say, "What a jerk!" Most people will take the money and give little more thought to it.

Social psychologists have some interesting observations about the illusion of control. Research demonstrates the general point that when people expend effort, they expect successful results. In one experiment, individuals were allowed to buy dollar lottery tickets with the chance of winning a large cash prize. Some were allowed to pick their own lottery numbers, and others were assigned lottery numbers. The researcher asked them later if they'd be willing to sell their lottery tickets. Those who picked their lottery numbers wanted far more money for their ticket than those whose numbers had been randomly assigned. Somehow, by merely picking the lottery numbers themselves, they developed an illusion that they stood a better chance of winning the lottery! (In fact, the odds of winning are the same whether you pick your number or have someone pick it for you.)

➡ **TAKE ACTION** ➡

Rate Your Control Power

Pick at least six situations in each day for the next month and predict your level of control. For each one write down:

1   The factors that will determine what happens in that situation.

2   What percentage of control you think you have.

3   The actual outcome.

4   The factors that really influenced what happened.

When you can predict 3 and 4 from 1 and 2 accurately, you'll know your judgment about control is good. This exercise is among the most important in this book. Practice it regularly.

PLAN FOR SUCCESS

The point I'm making is that you must learn to be deliberate about choosing in what (or in whom) you will invest your energy. You can't always know ahead of time whether you can succeed in something, and that's why life involves taking risks. But you

➡ **LOOK DEEPER**

When Should You Try to Control?

If you decide you have 80 percent control in a situation, is it a smart or foolish risk to try to make something happen? What about 70 percent? 50 percent? If you have only 20 percent control, but want to try anyway, will you be hurt less if it fails because you knew it was a long shot?

want to take smart risks, not foolish ones. That means you must anticipate just how much control you really have in a given situation.

Develop a True Perspective
The Balance of Control

From this discussion, you know that depression often arises from either attempting to control what can't be controlled or *not* controlling what can be controlled. No one is in control all the time, and everyone has control sometimes. The goals are to refine the way you recognize where the control really lies, *situation by situation,* and to develop a balanced perspective that keeps you from expending energy in a direction that simply cannot pay off. You must learn to use your energy intelligently when it is likely to produce the desired result. Remember, unless you have a deliberate plan for doing what you want to do, your efforts may be unfocused or misdirected. Once the failure dominoes begin to fall, you are at risk for depression. That's why I encourage you to have solid plans for doing things that matter to you. Insurance salespeople have a saying: "It isn't that people plan to fail, it's that they fail to plan."

Attempting to control every aspect of life is clearly no way to master it. Neither is missing obvious opportunities to take control over important things in your life. The right balance is evident when you walk away from a potentially hurtful situation because you recognize it's *outside* your control, and when you do invest energy and thought into a course of action because you know achieving the desired result is *within* your power. The exercises in this chapter are meant to sharpen your ability to recognize what is and is not in your control. If you know you can influence the outcome in a situation that is sufficiently important to justify your effort, then you must work to get the result you want. If, on the other hand, you see that no amount of your effort will bring success, you can deliberately choose to save your time and energy, thereby preventing frustration and depression.

The issue of control surfaces in your life many times a day, and you can't control that. But you can control whether you attempt to influence a situation, to what degree, and how clearly you define the point at which it's better to walk away than go down in flames.

KEY POINTS TO REMEMBER

- People have a basic need to control life situations, including other people.

- Depression often follows errors in judgment about the issues of control. The errors usually take one of two forms: either not controlling things that can be controlled, or trying to control things that cannot be controlled.

- Your perceptions about what can be controlled are the product of your experience and perceptions regarding whether you *make* things happen or whether things seem to happen *to* you.

- People who have tried to do something in one situation and failed can conclude, incorrectly, that they are helpless and then overgeneralize that failure to other unrelated situations. This is known as the illusion of helplessness.

- The belief that you can control the outcome of a situation when that control is beyond your influence is known as the illusion of control.

- The need to become very skilled at determining what is and is not in your control is highlighted by the fact that perceptions of control and depression are so closely related.

Chapter 7

GET CLEAR ABOUT BLAME, GUILT, AND YOUR RESPONSIBILITIES

Amanda rolled over, looked at the clock, and reluctantly decided it was time to get up. She started to get out of bed, but it took more effort than she was willing to expend, so she fell back on her pillow and slept some more. When she awoke a couple of hours later, Amanda was angry with herself for having slept so late. It wasn't that she really had to be up any earlier on Sunday, her one day off, but she was going to visit her mother. She knew her mother would make her feel terrible if she didn't get there early. Amanda chastised herself for being so self-indulgent.

Every other Sunday, Amanda drove 40 miles to her mother's retirement community to spend the day with her. She didn't mind so much when her dad was still alive, but since his death a year ago, these visits to her mother had become increasingly burdensome. She had loved her dad and had loved being with him because he was always so happy to see her and it was fun to be with him. Mom, on the other hand, was always stern and humorless. Talking to her was always a daunting, serious business, even when Amanda was just a little girl.

When her dad passed away, Amanda felt she lost a huge part of herself. Her mother had made some biting comments after the funeral. Now that Dad was gone, Amanda would probably not be coming to visit as much, she said, acknowledging snidely that she knew Amanda preferred her dad. Amanda had felt horrible when her mother said that, because it was true—and that made her feel even worse. Nevertheless, she had dutifully assured her mother she'd be out to see her just as often, maybe even more often. Since Mom was alone now, Amanda felt she should.

Every once in a while, Amanda wondered what her life would be like if her mother were dead. No sooner would the thought occur to her than Amanda would have an intense guilt attack for thinking something so awful. To atone for the thought, she'd make sure to pick up a gift for her mother, who placed great value on small gifts "that show you care." Amanda wondered how many gifts she'd given her mom over the years, starting with the very first—a potholder she made in first grade.

She became absorbed in this line of thought, remembering all the times her mother had made her feel guilty and undeserving over the years. One afternoon, she had accidentally locked herself out of the house and had gone to stay with a friend until someone got home. As she waited, Amanda got wrapped up in playing, and by the time she called home, her mother had already been looking for her frantically for half an hour. Her mother didn't talk to her for two weeks after that, acting as though Amanda were invisible. No matter how many times Amanda apologized, it wasn't enough.

THE NEVER-ENDING APOLOGY

It seemed that Amanda was always apologizing to her mother. She apologized for going off to college instead of marrying her mother-approved high school sweetheart. (Her mother thought he was God's gift to the world—so did he, unfortunately.) She apologized for getting a degree in political science instead of something more "womanly." She apologized for marrying one of her colleagues, and she apologized again four years later, when she announced her divorce. She was still apologizing for not remarrying and for not having children.

Amanda's whole life was one big apology to her mother and to herself, because no matter what she did, Amanda felt that somehow it wasn't right, not good enough. Yes, her mother had taught her guilt as a way of life, and Amanda learned the lesson well. She could feel guilty for eating well when children were starving someplace, or for ignoring a panhandler when she had money in her purse—anything that made her feel like she wasn't being or doing what she should.

Amanda abruptly broke this train of thought. She showered, dressed quickly, then drove to a card shop that also sold small gift items. She picked out a syrupy card (more acceptable than a funny one) and bought a little statuette as a gift. On her way out, Amanda called to tell her mother she was on her way and when she expected to arrive. "Oh," her mother remarked, obviously disappointed. "I thought you'd be here by now."

Do you feel guilty more often or more intensely than you know you should? A sense of excessive or inappropriate guilt is one of the classic patterns associated with clinical depression. This chapter will focus on the issues commonly associated with guilt. Specifically, you will learn how inappropriate guilt comes about and what you can do about it.

Guilt is strongly related to your sense of responsibility. The more you feel an obligation to satisfy the expectations of other people or to meet your own expectations, the more guilt you are likely to experience. Amanda's case represents this relationship quite well. Let's look at how we develop a sense of personal responsibility.

LEARNING THE HARD WAY

Because we're social beings, we all exist in a network of interpersonal relationships. This requires establishing specific

---

▶ **TAKE ACTION** ▶

Prepare Yourself for Difficult Choices

Even when everything is going well, it's a challenge to meet all of life's demands as parent, child, employee, citizen, and more. And when your obligations conflict, the need to make tough choices is bound to surface. You can ease the strain by trying to anticipate the decisions coming up and your most congenial responses to them.

Make a list of the different roles that you occupy in life. What expectations are associated with each role—what must you do or not do—to fulfill that role adequately? As you review all your roles, you may see conflicting expectations. How do you feel when you are caught between such demands?

---

roles and, along with those roles, specific expectations to carry out those roles adequately. Each of us has multiple roles to fill. You can be a father/mother, a husband/wife, an employee/employer, a son/daughter, and so forth, all at the same time. To expect all the different roles you play (and their associated expectations) to mesh smoothly at all times is obviously unrealistic. Inevitably, conflicts arise from the various demands associated with playing multiple roles at a given moment.

WHAT AM I GIVING? WHAT DO I GET?

One choice all of us face daily in each of our relationships is this: "How much do I do for you, and how much do I do for me?" If I value my relationship with you, I don't want to disappoint you and risk your disapproval. On the other hand, if I do things for you simply to get your approval or avoid conflict, I feel that I'm selling myself out, and that won't help my self-image.

It is stressful to decide whether to do something of importance for myself that may preclude my doing something for you. Should I lend you my car because you asked to borrow it? Or should I use it to run personal errands that are important to me? If I give you my car or do other such things for you at my own expense, I'm likely to grow resentful toward you and feel bad about myself, too. If I don't do such things for you, then I run the risk of your getting angry and withdrawing your approval from me. Either way, I face an unpleasant prospect: feel bad about myself or feel bad about you.

Your perceptions about personal responsibility are shaped by other people's expectations. The important people in your life shaped your sense of freedom to create a balance between meeting your own needs and your sense of duty to others. For example, some people are raised to avoid disappointing anyone, and the mechanism for that is guilt. This powerful manipulative tool really works—which is probably why it's so popular. It's also very destructive.

If your parents used guilt to get you to follow their wishes, you faced a heavy psychological penalty whenever you disappointed them. You didn't want to hurt your parents, the most important people in your life, in any way. Their approval counted for nearly everything. Such a childhood background makes you sensitive, perhaps too sensitive, to other people's reactions. If you feel it is your job to save others from their disappointment or frustration, you are an easy target for the guilt they place on you (and the guilt you place on yourself *for* them!).

HOW TO DEFEND YOURSELF AGAINST GUILT

Your best defense against guilt is a clear sense of the right thing to do in meeting your own needs and the expectations of others. Knowing what guilt is and where it comes from is a necessary step in protecting yourself from the manipulation by guilt others routinely use, often unwittingly.

LOOK DEEPER
Trace Your Introduction to Guilt

Were you raised to feel guilty? What type of pressure, and how much, was placed on you to feel guilty enough to do what was expected? Are you aware of other mechanisms that were used to manipulate your feelings to get the same compliance from you?

Remember Amanda? Can you see how her unrelenting guilt feelings could fuel depression? It's draining to live with the constant anxiety that you will be judged harshly and to have to deal with the disappointment, anger, or rejection of others you want to please. You give away your personal power when you allow others to determine whether you are worthy of their attention or affection. To get over crippling guilt—the kind that makes life (or certain aspects of it) painful—you must reclaim your right to be who you are and to live your life as you choose. The previous discussion and exercises regarding personal values will help you do this.

Beyond its connection to responsibility, guilt is also associated with fear. To the extent that you fear rejection or the

LOOK DEEPER
Delve into the Problem of Perfectionism

Are you a perfectionist? In what area(s) do you strive for perfection? Is it possible to achieve? If you attempt to live up to your definition of perfection, how will you feel when others disagree with your standard? When others define perfection for you and you can't live up to it, how does it make you feel? Do you see that this is a no-win situation?

withdrawal of affection if you do not do what others ask of you, you feel guilt if you think you're letting them down. To get rid of this guilt and the associated depression, you must begin to ask yourself, "If this person can reject me for not fulfilling her expectations, what kind of relationship is it?" Your goal is to be in relationships where people support you in your decisions and respect your need to do what you must do.

Beyond responsibility and fear, guilt also relates to perfectionism, a common theme in the lives of depressed individuals. To the rational mind, wanting to be perfect is entirely unrealistic. Even though most depressed people recognize the impossibility of achieving perfection, it doesn't excuse them from requiring it of themselves. Here's another example of the all-or-none thinking I described earlier. A lifetime of thinking you're either perfect or you're junk is a painful (and entirely distorted) existence.

➡ TAKE ACTION ➡

Make Peace with Your Mistakes

If you want to maintain good self-esteem and reduce your depression, you must learn to tolerate your mistakes without being mean to yourself. After all, you have a human body and a human mind, so like all of us, you will make mistakes as long as you live. The issue here is how to treat yourself fairly when you do make mistakes.

To learn how to handle your mistakes in a more positive, accepting way, try the exercise of making deliberate mistakes in harmless situations. Each day, make three obvious errors: get off the wrong freeway exit, mismatch your socks, call someone by the wrong name. Evaluate the results objectively. Do these mistakes damage the world? Is civilization as we know it affected? Does anything change? Of course not!

You don't have to like making mistakes, or encourage them in others. But if you can accept them when they happen and learn from them, it will help your self-image. Never abuse yourself for making a mistake.

Understanding the motivation behind perfectionism is not difficult. A perfect person risks no rejection or disapproval from others (except from those who feel uncomfortable and inadequate in the presence of perfection). Perfectionism is basic to the experience of depression, and I will discuss it in more detail later in this chapter.

HOW FAR SHOULD YOU GO FOR APPROVAL?

We are dependent on others as an inevitable part of growing up. How can we be indifferent to the reactions of those who raised us, the sources of our physical and emotional security? Normally, we can't. Anyone who is immune to the reactions of others is likely to be a pretty strange character.

I want to point out that there is a positive value in seeking approval from others. It is a means of attaining the strong bonds

---

➥ **TAKE ACTION** ➥

Examine Your Efforts to Earn Approval

What do you do to earn approval from others? Be very descriptive of the specific personality traits you use to elicit approval—generosity, praise, hard work, compliance. How well do these approval-seeking patterns work for you? When are they clearly advantageous—and disadvantageous? In your judgment, is your approval-seeking behavior more or less than is good for you? How do you know?

Here is one way to examine the effect pleasing others has on you. Exaggerate approval-seeking behaviors for a day by attempting to say and do things specifically designed to elicit the approval of others (unnecessary compliments, small gifts to people who are unimportant to you, fawning phone calls, and the like). How do you feel when you do this?

of closeness and support. It helps you in developing sensitivity and empathy, vital characteristics for a sense of social responsibility. It is also a basis for forming self-esteem. Seeking and obtaining approval reinforces us for the things we do and gives us an important basis for feeling worthwhile.

Even as adults, we build our lives around the values we learned as children, whether for career, family, or ethics. Like the excessive acceptance of guilt, the excessive drive for approval can be destructive. It's excessive if your need for approval is so strong that you compromise your own values to get it. If your need for approval consistently places you in the position of seeing yourself as less important than others, it is excessive.

MY MIND IS MADE UP ABOUT ME

Self-image is remarkably stable. Despite years of experience, a mature person can feel almost exactly the same about himself as he did in earliest childhood. The reason for this is *cognitive dissonance,* a concept introduced by psychologist Leon Festinger over 30 years ago. It describes the need people have to maintain stability in their belief systems by rejecting (ignoring or discounting) input that conflicts with preexisting beliefs. Once you have formed a self-image of who you are and what your relative worth is, will your self-image change if someone contradicts it? Or will you dismiss the value or accuracy of that person's observations about you?

Let's put this point into a real-life context. Sam views himself as an honest person. He goes to see his accountant, who asks him to explain a large tax deduction for treating a huge number of people (too many to be true) to business lunches. By questioning Sam's truthfulness concerning the deduction, the accountant challenges Sam's view of himself as an honest person. Of course, Sam's first reaction is annoyance at being asked to justify himself. His next reaction is to defend the deduction by offering endless rationalizations: "Everyone cheats on income taxes. Why should I pay when big business gets all the breaks? Why should I contribute my money to build nuclear weapons?" Will Sam's image of himself be different when he leaves his accountant's office? Of course not. Sam will see himself as an honest person and merely ignore the fact that he has done something that was clearly dishonest.

Have you ever heard a debate where one person abandons her position at the end and says, "Okay, now I see it your way"? Not likely! Instead, both debaters become entrenched even further in their original positions, regardless of any new information or new perspectives put forth by the opponent.

Cognitive dissonance is a neutral mechanism—not good or bad; its role is to maintain the stability of your experience, whatever the merit of it. If you have a bad self-image, you either disregard positive feedback altogether or minimize its importance. If your self-image is positive, you simply discount your critics as lacking insight into your true value.

Cognitive dissonance as a mechanism for maintaining stability does much to explain how people limit themselves unnecessarily and unwittingly. This device encourages you to reinforce your own limitations. Here's how it works: If you think of yourself as unlovable (not attractive, smart, sexy, or desirable), you are unlikely to respond positively to interest from others, simply because such interest in you contradicts your self-image. If someone shows you affection, you are likely to question his motives: "Why is this person trying to be nice to me? Does he feel sorry for me? Is he trying to use me in some way?" In rejecting affection from others, you do not experience being loved, and that confirms your original belief that you are not lovable!

How is that for a self-limiting pattern? How about letting others decide how they feel about you rather than trying to do their thinking for them? If someone finds you desirable, even though you don't understand why, that person has the right to feel that way.

Consider another example. If you see yourself as helpless in life, you won't put forth any meaningful effort to change things for the better. So you let circumstances control you rather than trying to control circumstances yourself, which confirms that you are a helpless victim of circumstances!

This point is so important that I'll provide still a third example: If you see the future as negative, and you feel hopeless about its ever being different, you won't do anything to change the future. That means things you don't like about the present will continue uninterrupted. Of course, you then experience more of the same, confirming your original belief.

How do you get out of such vicious cycles? Clearly, the emphasis throughout this book is on the need to *do something different*. I am stating in no uncertain terms that because of the distorted patterns of perception associated with your depression, you cannot trust your judgment 100 percent yet.

Hopefully, as you become practiced in balancing your internal perceptions with external realities, your judgment will become much more reliable. At this point, however, I stress the need for you to work toward reading situations more accurately. Then you will be able to respond to each one on its own merits, with the best response available in that situation.

The factor of cognitive dissonance is also the reason why I cannot overemphasize the need to do the exercises suggested throughout this book. Just reading these exercises is not enough;

➙ **LOOK DEEPER**

Do You Work at Self-Improvement?

Have you been participating in these exercises throughout the book? If not, how do you explain the apparent contradiction between your wanting to get over depression and your unwillingness to do what it takes to master the skills necessary to do it? If you take the time to answer this question seriously, you will see how cognitive dissonance involves working very hard to stay the same.

only by doing them do you get the intended impact. Unless you have a strong experience that challenges your beliefs about yourself in a powerful way, it is too easy to maintain the attitudes you have now.

WHEN ONE *NO* BEATS A HUNDRED *YESES*

Sometimes even people who have direct feedback manage to discount it. For example, the person who addresses 100 people can give a wonderful speech as far as the group is concerned, yet still feel bad because he has convinced himself that he did poorly. Even with the 99 out of 100 written evaluations by people who rate the presentation excellent, the one rating of fair monopolizes the speaker's mind, so he sees the entire presentation as unsuccessful.

This knack depressed individuals have—finding and amplifying the tiniest negative in even the most positive situations—is called selective perception. The all-or-none pattern of distorted thinking leads you to conclude that unless something is 100 percent successful, it is a complete failure. Unfortunately, the mechanism of cognitive dissonance stabilizes this pattern of depressed thinking. Unless you actively seek new experiences to overload your perceptions, you can easily discount every exception and maintain your original depressing viewpoint.

IS IT BAD TO DO WHAT'S BEST FOR *YOU*?

In the earlier discussion of interacting with others to enjoy the benefits of acceptance and avoid the pain of rejection, you saw that not everyone responds to others in the same way. Why? The single most important factor seems to be self-image. People with high self-esteem are more likely to take responsibility for themselves and let others do the same. They don't feel the need to control others, rescue others, or find others to lean on.

➡ **TAKE ACTION** ➡

Better Your Image

Think of specific feedback you received in recent months that contradicts what you believe about yourself. How did you reject or discount that feedback? What kind of feedback would it take for you to revise your self-image?

On a blank sheet of paper, set up three columns. In one column write a statement about your self-image, and in the next column a behavior that contradicts it. In a third column, show how you could improve the behavior in your second column.

My Self-Image	Contradictory Behavior	Improvement Plans
I'm a responsible person.	I'm late for meetings and appointments.	I'll set out earlier to be on time.
I'm a good husband.	I never take the time to chat with my wife, though I know it would please her.	I'll engage in personal conversation daily, with no outside interruptions permitted.

Does it sound selfish for individuals to be guided more by their needs than the needs of others? How is being selfish different from taking care of yourself? Those most prone to guilt are usually unclear about the distinction. They often feel that doing things for their own benefit or responding to their own needs is bad—selfish, therefore wrong. If you have been brought up to put other people first, doing things for yourself will feel wrong and give rise to guilt. If others discover this about you, you become an easy target for manipulation.

Naturally, other people want what they want. Their wants may even be realistic. The question is, Must they get what they want at your expense?

↪ **LOOK DEEPER**

Examine Your Right to Say No

Think of people who recently asked you to do things for them. Were there times when you declined? If so, was it simple selfishness, or were you taking care of yourself? How do you know?

THE BLAME DODGERS

Thus far, the focus has been on people who develop such a strong sense of responsibility that they accept levels of guilt that are both unnecessary and inappropriate. What about the other type of person who shows no sense of responsibility, either for self or others? Such people rarely feel guilty even when they should. Their system is to blame others for their problems. They blame the weather, the economy, the government, their parents—anything or anyone to avoid taking responsibility for their own screwups. (Actually, those individuals probably aren't reading this book. After all, it encourages taking responsibility for yourself and initiating action for structured self-help.)

If you tend to feel guilt easily, you are vulnerable to abuse by such irresponsible people. The abuse comes when you assume that because *you* feel guilt and responsibility, others do, too. (I hope that by now you are learning not to use your views as the only reference point for interpreting the behavior of others.) In fact, I assure you that many individuals avoid responsibility and are very well practiced at blaming others for their problems.

It is easy to appreciate how happy a "blamer" is when she finds someone who has an overdeveloped sense of guilt and accepts blame without question. Obviously, you need to have a refined ability to sort out what you are and are not responsible for, situation by situation. This allows you to avoid accepting inappropriate blame or guilt.

JUST WHAT *ARE* YOU RESPONSIBLE FOR?

When you believe that something is within your control, you feel responsible for the outcome. If you don't get what you want, feelings of guilt and inadequacy creep in. If this happens to you now and then, it's time to develop a new decision-making process. *Before* you allow yourself to feel guilty or inadequate about not getting the outcome you desire, pause and make an evaluation: Was your strategy—the sequence of steps you took—inappropriate in some way (which suggests learning to do something else, developing a new strategy)? Or was the lack of success due to an illusion of control—thinking you could control something that was beyond you (which suggests the need to get clear about what is and is not within your control)?

In acknowledging the possibility that guilt can distort your perceptions about responsibility in a given situation, I am directly saying that you need to evaluate your role as each situation arises. We know distortions will take place (in varying degrees) in two forms: the tendency to be underresponsible for others and for things that happen, and the tendency to be overresponsible for others and for things that happen.

➡ TAKE ACTION ➡

Determine Where Duty Stops

Go back to Amanda's story at the start of this chapter. Identify what Amanda felt she had to do to please her mother. After each item you find, decide whether Amanda really was responsible for it. For example, she felt guilty about marrying someone her mother didn't like. Was she really responsible for getting her mother's approval? (I hope you said no.) Examine the other duties Amanda took on and think about the problem of overresponsibility.

IT'S NOT MY FAULT!

Those who show patterns of underresponsibility continually see themselves as victims of circumstances. They do this by failing to anticipate how they might be affected by their choices or those others make. Then they are quick to blame others for whatever problem befalls them. For example, the husband of one couple I worked with would say terribly mean things to his wife during their arguments. Naturally, she would be hurt by his vicious words. When the argument was over, he expected her to be warm and friendly, as though nothing had happened. When she couldn't do that, he blamed her for being unable to control her anger. How's that for the ability to avoid being at fault?

Here are some patterns common to those who don't deal realistically with issues of personal responsibility.

Speak Up or Feel Shot Down

Many depressed individuals can't express their thoughts, feelings, and needs. Some feel that speaking out would seem like a selfish bid for attention. Others fear that if they open up, they will be rejected. Finally, some simply don't know what they think or feel.

The main problem with not communicating your thoughts and feelings is that it puts you in the victim role. The person you are dealing with automatically handles the situation from her perspective only. No matter how sensitive that person might be, unless she is a mind reader, she will miss opportunities to take your feelings into account. Then you may get depressed, interpreting her actions as evidence that you are not valued or appreciated.

I know of no bona fide mind readers on this planet, so it is imperative that you tell others how you feel and what you want. If you don't do that and the other person does declare what he or she wants, you end up feeling overruled. Such interactions

Do People Know How You Feel?

Do you express your feelings? Or do you assume that other people know how you feel? Among the families I work with, Mom and/or Dad rarely say "I love you" or "I'm proud of you" to their children. In family therapy sessions where I encourage the expression of warm feelings toward each other, I am dismayed to be told frequently, "My daughter knows I love her. Why must I tell her?"

Do not assume other people know how you feel. If you want your feelings to be known, accept the responsibility of making sure they are.

leave you feeling helpless and trapped, and they encourage all the depressed thoughts and feelings that make the situation difficult to handle. Do you see how one thing (not expressing yourself) leads to another (feeling devalued), which then leads to another (feeling depressed)? That's the snowball effect of depression.

One precautionary note: Simply telling someone what you want does *not* obligate that person to fulfill your desire; it simply lets the other person know what it is. Of course, unless the other person knows what you want, you stand *no* chance of getting it. Likewise, someone's telling you what he or she wants does *not* obligate you to fulfill that desire. That's the point about equality in a relationship; it means hashing things out with each other until you arrange something *both* can live with.

Being afraid to display your feelings because someone will disagree with or even discount them is an act of underresponsibility. It means that you have decided not to operate as an equal in the relationship. You may be right about the other person. He *may* discount you. If so, it's time to redefine that relationship and assert the importance of your feelings. When you place yourself in the one down position, you effectively put the other person in the one up position. A relationship that is lopsided cannot function in a healthy way.

You Choose (and I'll Hate It)

I have a close friend who used to make going out to eat together very difficult. Every time I would ask, "Where would you like to eat?" she would respond, "Anywhere is fine. It doesn't matter." Her passive response would make me responsible for choosing the restaurant. Almost every time, no matter what place I chose, she would make thinly veiled complaints about it after we were inside and ready to eat. I had several choices. I could have:

- Let that pattern go on and let my resentment about it rise.
- Confronted her and expressed my anger about it.
- Stopped going out to eat with her.
- Tried to engage her in the selection process

Well, rather than get too angry over the situation, I decided instead to do something to get her involved in choosing the restaurant. The next time I asked her where she wanted to go and she replied, "Anywhere is fine," I took her to the most run-down, unattractive, aesthetically appalling restaurant I could find—and it had a miserable menu to boot. I did it with a sense of humor, and she was truly moved by the experience.

Now when I ask her where she would like to eat, she is quick to state her preference! I state my preference, too. If we disagree on both of those choices, we discuss alternatives and arrive at a satisfying compromise.

The only time it's important to assert your feelings and desires is when they matter to the course of the relationship. Insensitive as it may sound, there will be times when your feelings are simply irrelevant to the circumstances. Part of developing a clear sense of responsibility is knowing when it's important to speak up and when voicing your feelings is irrelevant. Sometimes

---

> ➡️ **TAKE ACTION** ➡️
>
> ## Start to Speak Up
>
> Scary as it might seem to you, only experience will show you how to assert your feelings and have them count in decisions with others. You will not always get your way, but you will be an equal in the decision-making process. Identify situations you care about where you have not made a point of expressing your values and preferences, and take a stand. Start with simple ones, such as places you like to eat or when you want to meet, and slowly progress to more difficult situations.

expressing yourself may simply feel good to you, even if you know it probably won't change things. The aim is to have a range of choices for the best response in a given situation.

I'm Angry (but I Shouldn't Be)

It's surprising to see how frequently people discount their own feelings. They state their reaction to a situation and then exclaim, "But I have no right to feel this way." Such self-negation really misses the mark in managing the situation well. Your saying "I have no right to feel this way" is irrelevant, since you obviously *do* feel that way. Your claim that there is no reasonable basis for your feelings cuts into your ability to resolve those feelings.

Let's put this idea into a real-life situation. Imagine a couple arguing about finances, and one says, "It makes me very angry that you want to spend money on something so silly." The other responds, "You have no right to feel angry! After all, it's my money, too." If I were the therapist working with this couple, I would interrupt them right there. To the person who said, "You have no right to feel angry," I would point out that the comment is irrelevant, since the other person *does* feel angry. Discussing whether the angry feeling is justified doesn't address the feeling itself, nor does it show any understanding of it. How should you best respond to the angry feelings already there?

Attempting to justify your feelings raises the question, What is proper justification for feeling angry, hurt, or happy? The answer is that you don't have to justify any feelings. They are spontaneous expressions of your nature. I don't encourage you to put your feelings first in every situation, because at times your feelings will be distorted and misleading (inappropriate to the context). But it is important to note each feeling, to have control over *whether* you express that feeling, and if so, how and to what degree.

You can recognize feelings without necessarily expressing them. For example, you know you're angry with your boss for overloading you with unnecessary work, but you also know that expressing your anger would not sit well with her. In such a case, you might wisely choose to acknowledge the feelings to yourself but not express them. Or, just as wisely, you might choose to meet with your boss and express your feelings in a nondefensive and nonthreatening way. The point is: You must assess your feelings intelligently and deal with them according to what the situation requires and what the other person can handle. Simply dumping your feelings can aggravate an already sensitive situation.

Denying your feelings is virtually opposite to everything I advocate in this book. I encourage you to recognize, accept, and utilize your feelings in a systematic way. Organize them according to your internal perceptions as well as the external realities of a given situation. Then decide whether expressing them is constructive. Instead of automatically being in touch with your feelings and impulsively expressing them, there will be times when the best choice is to get *out of touch* with your feelings!

Okay, Have It Your Way (but Be Prepared to Lose)

Most people respond to situations or individuals according to how they feel or what they want. Too often they respond without reading the person or situation very well.

LOOK DEEPER

Figure Out Why Things Go Wrong

Think about specific situations you faced recently that did not go well. What factors did you not take into account in each situation? The other person's values, the organization's policies, the influence of previous traditions, expectations of others? Will you be able to take more factors into account when you read a situation in the future?

Suppose you use *your* values, *your* rules for behavior, and *your* expectations as the guidelines for what *should* happen in dealing with people or events. Do you miss cues in the person or situation that can tell you they are operating on a different set of principles? To focus on your internal needs and wants to the exclusion of external realities puts you in a hazardous position because you don't consider all of the variables in deciding on the most effective thing to do. That's when mistakes are commonly made.

ANOTHER DISASTER: *YOU* DID IT AGAIN!

Blaming others for things that happen or don't happen is a prominent characteristic of underresponsible people. If they can blame others, they can claim to be the victim of someone else's incompetence. Many of these individuals are expert at getting other people to take responsibility. That way, if something goes wrong, the blame lands on someone else. (Remember my restaurant-selection friend? She blamed me for making bad choices, although she refused to make a choice herself.)

Learning to accept your fair share of responsibility means realizing that you don't always behave perfectly. As you make the inevitable mistakes we all make, you become more effective

---

➡ **TAKE ACTION** ➡

Don't Repeat Your Errors

Learning from your mistakes means analyzing past errors so you can prevent repeating them. Focus on a half dozen recent errors you made that aren't upsetting to you. For each one, ask yourself what factors contributed to the error. Should you have considered your feelings more or less? Were you overinformed or underinformed? Identify specific mechanisms for improved handling of similar situations in the future.

---

as a problem-solver and as a visionary of probable consequences. You may not be able to eliminate mistakes from your life, but when you do make them, you'll know it's not due to stupidity, incompetence, or anything else to blame yourself for.

I'M NOT HERE

A particularly disturbing aspect of depression is the withdrawal from life situations. It's common for people caught in the grip of depression to stop expending the effort to seek out new experiences. In severe cases, the person may not even respond to everyday things like a ringing telephone or a knock at the door. The more you isolate yourself when you are depressed, the deeper your limitations become. When you withdraw from people and situations, you assume a position of surrender; you roll over and play dead, admitting to yourself that you are a victim of forces too powerful to deal with. You must realize that the idea is *not* just to expend energy when you're depressed but to expend it wisely to achieve a goal. It's not enough to take an exercise class or volunteer at the hospital (although those are pretty good ideas). I say that instead of withdrawing, which can only complicate matters, you should take active and deliberate steps to interrupt the hurtful patterns and to build the helpful ones.

IT *MUST* BE MY FAULT!

An underresponsible individual is too quick to blame others, but an overresponsible person is too quick to accept blame. Also, the overresponsible individual is likely to consider the feelings of others at the expense of his own. If you find yourself frequently caught up in the lives of others, either by being drawn in or perhaps butting in, you're overresponsible. Let others live their lives. Make yourself a model of how to live well.

It is easy to see how some people become overresponsible. Along with family dynamics, culture plays a role in encouraging that characteristic in many of us. A good example is the so-called higher-consciousness groups that have emerged in recent years. I find their exaggerated emphasis on personal responsibility destructive. Such groups strongly influence many who don't perceive how unrealistic their teachings are. This includes all too many members of *my* profession.

Some of these groups flatly state, "You are responsible for *everything* that occurs in your life and for everything that happens around you. The events of your life are a reflection of you." Such an extreme viewpoint suggests that if someone hits your car from behind while you're waiting at a stop sign, you are somehow responsible for creating the energy that made the accident possible!

This view of responsibility has spilled over into health care. Many advocate the philosophy that your health is entirely up to you. They teach that the onset of cancer and other life-threatening disease is the patient's personal responsibility. They will tell such patients, "You created your cancer. It results from anger not appropriately expressed to the significant people in your life. You will be able to cure your cancer when you have resolved those issues." That the person has cancer is bad enough, but he is also blamed for causing it!

My deep involvement in the field of clinical hypnosis has taught me a great deal about the relationship between mind and body. I have a great respect for the mind's ability to affect physical processes. However, the extreme and overly simplistic position that emotions directly cause cancer blatantly disregards numerous other variables that contribute to the disease process. A patient looking for a way to explain the onset of his cancer may accept the claim that angry emotions caused the cancer simply because it answers the question, Why? I find such simplistic cause/effect statements by health professionals irresponsible. Further, I object to the way such statements can blur the truth about what a person is and is not responsible for.

BRING ME YOUR POOR . . .

Learning to define and respect the limits of your responsibility is necessary for managing your life—and your depression—well. I know this is not as easy as it sounds. Consider those of us in the mental health profession, for example. Many psychiatrists, psychologists, counselors, social workers, and the like are not doing well in the mental health department themselves. Being responsible for the health care of others is stressful in itself. Also, it is difficult to find a balance for yourself when you genuinely care about the welfare of others—the reason that you go into the health profession in the first place. However, unless you learn to establish a firm upper limit on how much you can care about others, it is easy to lose your sense of internal balance and become overresponsible for others.

Some of my colleagues are happy when their clients are doing well and miserable when they're not. Some lend money to their clients, and many get overinvolved in every decision their clients make. In general, the lives of these professionals are too enmeshed in the lives of the people they are trying to help. They lose their objectivity, their emotions ride a roller coaster, and their judgment becomes clouded about their client's best interest.

If educated and experienced mental health professionals sometimes find it difficult to establish the limits of responsibility, you can see why an untrained person can run into problems. Whatever your profession, whatever your station in life, the tricky question of responsibility calls for constant reassessment.

Guilt presupposes responsibility; you don't feel guilty if you don't feel responsible. To diminish the power of guilt in your life, you must learn to establish realistic expectations for yourself. Give yourself the kind of extra consideration you willingly give others, and clarify the expectations of others. Identify where your expectations of yourself came from and how others get you to meet their expectations. Then *you* can decide whether you want to continue meeting expectations you didn't create.

Of course, the expectations that go along with the roles you play will always be there. You must consider exactly how you will balance them with your own knowledge of what makes you feel best. The more you can resist the desire to satisfy others at your own expense, the more others will start to be responsible

---

➡ TAKE ACTION ➡

Reassess Your Responsibilities

Whom do you feel responsible for in your life? What do you do for these people as a result of this feeling? Could they start to do these things for themselves? If it seems reasonable to you, talk to the people about the specific responsibilities you feel they can handle and why. Get their reaction to your attitude. Do they confirm it, or do their answers change your viewpoint in some way? Can you see why they might want you to continue taking responsibility for them even if it's not in your best interest?

for themselves. Encourage the people around you to get their needs met in ways that aren't destructive to others (like you).

PERFECTIONISM IS A TICKET TO APPROVAL

Perfectionists set exceptionally high standards for themselves and are intensely critical of themselves when they do not reach these standards. Perfectionism reflects the distortion of extreme all-or-none thinking. For example, I remember treating an athlete who won a silver medal at the Olympics but convinced himself he was a total failure because he didn't win the gold. If that is not evidence of all-or-none thinking, I don't know what is.

For the underresponsible individual, perfectionism is a guaranteed way of attaining approval from others, and that means avoiding blame, judgment, and criticism at the same time. For this person in particular, the perfectionistic standards are usually not even her own. Instead, she has some Significant Other (real or imagined) who sets the criteria for success. In other words, she imagines how someone important will react to something she does and behaves according to what she thinks is most likely to get approval.

A lot of doctors, for example, became doctors simply to avoid disappointing their parents. Living to avoid the criticism or disappointment of others is a hollow existence. It represents underresponsibility to yourself and an overresponsibility toward others.

You must come up with your own definition of success. Even if it is different from what others call success, it is your right and your *obligation* to do what is best for *you* if you truly want long-term relief from depression. By trying to live up to the standards others set, you hurt yourself from within, so you must set standards based on your own values. You do not strive for perfection to avoid the judgments of others or to attain their approval, but to establish *realistic* expectations for yourself. Learning to set limits on the judgments of others is a much more constructive

LOOK DEEPER

Define Your Own Success

If you tend toward perfectionism, ask yourself, "What is my definition of success? Who established this standard?" If it was anyone but you, you aren't really in control of your own life!

response than negating your personal needs to meet their expectations.

Perfectionism can also be clearly related to tendencies of overresponsibility. Challenging yourself never to disappoint others is an undeniably responsible position to take. Be aware, though, that taking on such a responsibility can lead to high, demanding, and worst of all, never-ending expectations. It's like being a parent who continues to do things for a child long after the child knows how to do them for himself. In essence, the child is being told, "There is no need for you to do this yourself because I will do it for you." Continuing to do things for others reinforces their perception that they don't need to do those things for themselves.

For every overresponsible person there is also someone who is underresponsible. If you burden yourself unfairly by doing

LOOK DEEPER

When Can Help Be a Hindrance?

Is it ever harmful to help someone? Think of specific things you do to help the important people in your life. Do they take it for granted? How did it happen that you became responsible for those things? Does it work to the advantage of the relationship or not?

things that could be balanced by having others do more, you will eventually feel overwhelmed and then resentful that you are being taken for granted. The hardest thing to do in working with overresponsible people is to teach them to let other people be responsible for themselves! They see this as abandoning or burdening others, shirking their own responsibilities.

In fact, when you encourage others to take over the things that you were doing for them, you foster a more mature and equal relationship that will ultimately prove more satisfying. Initially, of course, the person is likely to grumble a bit about taking on new responsibilities. But both of you will survive it and be the better for it.

STAY AWAY FROM THE DANCE-FASTER POSITION

Another aspect of this issue concerns the illusion of control, which has you thinking that you can *make* someone proud, happy, or secure. This presupposes you have an ability to control others. But we know that illusion creates unrealistic demands and expectations. By striving to satisfy another, you make that person the judge of how effectively you are meeting his needs. It means that person can push you to try harder and harder as he becomes increasingly critical of you.

Amanda, the woman whose story began this chapter, illustrates the point about expectations and resentment. The stress, the resentment, and the depression you experience in a dance-faster position worsens every day you keep dancing. Until Amanda sets limits on her mother's expectations, she will be on the treadmill of increasing demands, with no real acknowledgment of her efforts. To her mother, Amanda will never be the perfect daughter.

The desire to be perfect at something or to excel at something is a double-edged sword. Clearly, it motivates achievement and results in recognition and reward. These rewards breed the need to be *more* perfect. The downside is that you are forced to achieve higher and higher levels of excellence, to the point where success itself becomes a depressing trap.

This is why so many highly successful individuals are depressed. They are so good at what they do that the continual

---

KEY POINTS TO REMEMBER

- Excessive or inappropriate guilt is a common feature of clinical depression.
- Guilt is strongly related to your sense of personal responsibility for meeting the expectations of others.
- Guilt is a manipulative tactic to encourage compliance.
- Your need to rise to the expectations others have of you is determined by your level of self-esteem.
- The term *cognitive dissonance* describes the way people strive to maintain stability in their beliefs by discounting any information that conflicts with these beliefs.
- There is an important difference between being selfish and taking care of yourself.
- A distorted sense of responsibility leads you to either deny responsibility you should accept or accept responsibility when you should refuse it.
- It is essential to develop a clear sense of what you are and are not responsible for. Then you can manage guilt feelings appropriately, thereby reducing your depression.
- Among the numerous patterns associated with underresponsibility are lack of self-expression, negation of feelings, withdrawal, and blaming others.
- Perfectionism can result from either overresponsibility or underresponsibility.
- Learning to accept mistakes and correct them is necessary for healthy self-esteem.

striving for new achievement leaves them little room to enjoy the everyday aspects of life. Since no life is continuously exciting or challenging, getting comfortable with everyday living is basic to feeling good, but perfectionists are robbed of that. Instead, they continuously think about what to do next and how to do it better.

It's important to discover what your individual values and needs are, regardless of the expectations of others. Obviously, you cannot ignore the demands of others altogether. As a member of society, you have a responsibility to conduct yourself with integrity. On the other hand, if you consistently ignore your own needs in favor of doing what others expect, you put yourself on the path to depression. Live according to the standards you set for yourself. No one should be responsible for you and your feelings at his expense, and the reverse is equally true.

Chapter 8

SEE HOW YOUR BELIEFS CAN HURT YOU

You know from previous chapters that certain belief systems are generally associated with depression. Now I will discuss specific thought processes and attitudes that are likely to cause and maintain depression. A careful look at these common but potentially damaging attitudes will make you more aware of your own beliefs and the true effect they have on your life. Then you can decide on the circumstances that let your beliefs work in your favor and those that can lead to negative and potentially depressing consequences.

DEPRESSED PEOPLE MAKE COMMON ERRORS IN THINKING

Along with other experts, Aaron Beck, M.D., a well-known psychiatrist who studied the thought patterns of depressed individuals for more than 30 years, observed that depressed people frequently make errors in interpreting experience. So Dr. Beck devised a system, cognitive therapy, for identifying these errors, or distortions, and correcting them. You will recognize many of these ten common errors in thinking that can lead to or intensify depression. You will learn what they can mean in your life and how you can conquer them.

1 All-or-none (dichotomous) thinking
2 Overgeneralization
3 Mental filter (selective perception)
4 Disqualifying the positive
5 Jumping to conclusions
6 Magnification (catastrophizing) or minimization (trivializing)
7 Emotional reasoning
8 *Should* statements
9 Labeling and mislabeling
10 Personalization

Each of the distortions on Dr. Beck's list represents the interpretation of information and experience in a way that encourages depressed feelings. To start with, he considers your emotions to be the direct consequence of your perceptions. Following that line of thinking, you're encouraged to deal with things that go on in your life in a rational way as a remedy for depression. Rationality means thinking clearly, weighing the evidence of facts for your conclusions, and keeping your feelings in line with reality. The theory is that large doses of rationality can cure most episodes of depression and prevent many others. Let's look at each of the cognitive distortions.

The All-or-None Attitude
Dichotomous Thinking

All-or-none thinkers see things in terms of black and white, with little or no gray in between. Such a person gets a B on an exam and feels like a failure; he misses out on a promotion at work and feels like a loser; she fails to get unanimous approval for some accomplishment and sees herself as a reject. Whenever you let a small unpleasantness ruin an entire experience, you show at least some evidence of all-or-none thinking.

You may recall from chapter 5 that such extreme thinking is related to a low tolerance for frustration and ambiguity. People like clarity and certainty; confusion is very unsettling. A lack of certainty about the best response to a situation or the meaning of something creates a sense of urgency to get things straight. As you strive to get a clear understanding as quickly as possible, you may make errors in judgment that may prove quite costly.

Pressure Sensitivity

Think of a real-life situation in which a woman in a dating relationship wants to get a commitment from the man she has been seeing for several months. If he is unsure about his feelings or about the wisdom of making a commitment, he probably won't make any promises to her. This leaves the woman uncertain about how he really feels.

To resolve the doubt, she is likely to increase the pressure for a commitment. But the extra pressure she exerts makes him think she is too anxious to get married, and it scares him. He tries to leave things a little looser, and she interprets that as a lack of caring. The woman ups the pressure and the man breaks off the relationship. Her uncertainty led to a demand for clarification, and the undesirable result was a breakup. Would the breakup have occurred anyway? Maybe—but maybe not.

You can find an individual interpretation for almost everything that happens in life from almost every person living it. Some views are valid, some are not. But it's clear that there are *many* right ways, all of them effective in achieving a desired result. However, all-or-none thinkers typically search for the *one* right way to manage life. But the truth is that few situations in life are all or none. Adjusting positively to life means recognizing the many shades of good, normal, right, and moral.

→ **LOOK DEEPER**

Do You Need to Lighten Up?

Thanksgiving day is ruined for Terry if there's no oyster dressing with the dinner. A poor dance partner for one waltz can wreck the entire evening for Aunt May. Without his usual chair at a meeting, Dad simply refuses to participate.

What are you extreme about in your thinking? Is it only in one area of your life, or in a variety of areas? How can you tell when you are being too black-and-white in your thinking? (The clue—you decide that something can be only one way, or it's no good.)

When you can accept that two individuals living virtually opposite lives can both still be right, you make a forward leap in thinking that allows for judging others and yourself much more generously. As you make the critic in your head lighten up a bit, more of what you do seems perfectly all right, even though it differs from your idea of perfection or the way you used to do things.

They're All Alike, So I Hate Them All
Overgeneralization

When you let one experience represent an entire class of experiences for you, you're overgeneralizing. Making a racial slur on the basis of a bad experience with a single individual demonstrates this type of erroneous thinking.

In the world of those who are depressed, overgeneralization surfaces when a person forms a broad conclusion and nonselectively applies it to all similar situations. If you have a particular type of negative experience, you have two choices: Recognize it as a singular event; or use it as the measure of your worth as an individual ("I'm no good"), the value of life ("Life stinks"), and all unpleasant situations ("It always happens this way").

When you overgeneralize, you demonstrate a lack of ability to recognize how situation B is different from situation A. Suppose you suffer a hurtful experience in a romantic relationship and you conclude that *all* men (or women) are cruel or selfish. You are obviously overgeneralizing. You can't really know that *all* men and *all* women are like this one person who hurt you.

At the breakup of a relationship, some people literally decide that "you can't trust women (or men), so I will never fall in love again." They build their lives around that overgeneralization, and years later they are still alone, still miserable. The solution lies in discriminating between situations, recognizing that each one must be judged on its own merit.

In the earlier example of the broken romance, seeing *all* men as noncommittal or *all* women as overanxious is an obvious distortion. The reasonable thing to do: Learn to be a better judge of whom to be involved with and whom to avoid. The range of men and women out there runs from wonderful to terrible. You must learn to tell them apart, considering each on individual merit. (You'll find some tips on how to do that in the next

---

Are You Fair to Others?   ➡ **LOOK DEEPER**

Are you prejudiced? In what ways do you think of or treat all members of a group as if they were the same? What experiences of yours have led you to overgeneralize feelings of helplessness, negative self-worth, and similar depressive patterns? How do people overcome prejudice? What can you do to explore the possibility that you are better than you give yourself credit for? *Do it!*

chapter.) If you follow the one-size-fits-all pattern of thinking, you are sure to make repeated mistakes that fuel negativity, poor self-esteem, and depression.

Have you noticed how difficult it is to overcome prejudices? Well, consider your poor self-image as a prejudice against yourself. If you have concluded that you are helpless, or incompetent, or anything of the kind, challenge that view of yourself. Go out of your way to do things that will alter that view. For example, if you see yourself as incapable of learning new things, sign up for classes in something that interests you, and note the discoveries you make as the course progresses.

Blinders Firmly in Place
Mental Filter

If you focus on one aspect of experience to the exclusion of other relevant details, you are using a mental filter. When a depressed individual focuses on the dark side of nearly everything, it can only cause negative feelings. First you must learn to address the mechanism of a mental filter effectively. Reduce your depression by recognizing that your automatic reaction to situations and people is likely to be negative. Now, challenge yourself to move beyond that first response by literally going out of your way to find the neutral or even positive aspects of that same situation or person.

As you become practiced in overcoming the mental filter, you will find that you do this almost automatically. For example, if a cashier shortchanges you in the grocery store, you can react by deciding that the cashier is dishonest and trying to take advantage of you. But you can also think of neutral (too busy) or even positive (rushing to serve you) possibilities for why you were shortchanged. Notice the difference in your feelings as you move from negative to neutral to positive interpretations.

➡️ **TAKE ACTION** ➡️

Learn to Explain Events Positively

Since there are less hurtful, even harmless explanations for an ambiguous event, why is it that your first explanation for it is a negative one? Challenge yourself to create a variety of explanations for each interaction in your day, rather than settle on a negative one. Here's an exercise.

Think of three ambiguous events or interactions you experienced this week that bothered you. On paper, describe the event objectively. Then write at least one positive and one neutral alternative viewpoint of the same experience. Here's how to do it.

What Actually Happened	Positive Interpretation	Neutral Interpretation
Mom refused to lend me money.	She's setting effective limits for her own well-being and wants me to be more independent.	She has to be more careful of how she spends money.

It's Only Right If It's Wrong
Disqualifying the Positive

Most of us tend to reject positive input from others by devaluing its worth or somehow ignoring its significance. In general, we tend to discount anything that contradicts our preexisting belief system. Remember the term *cognitive dissonance,* used to describe a person's response to life in a patterned and consistent manner as a way to keep his world stable? It is predictable that a depressed person whose belief system is negative will discount the positive. Someone who is optimistic is just as likely to reject any negative feedback.

When your negative beliefs go unchallenged, cognitive dissonance can keep you depressed, just as it can maintain happiness in others. If you have a poor image of yourself and someone tells you something positive but you don't accept it, you are left with only the negative. That means your self-image continues to be negative.

Break the negative cycle by starting with simple things. When someone pays you a compliment ("That's a nice dress"), simply say thank you. Don't let yourself discount the compliment. ("This old thing? I've had it for years.") You can let others appreciate you, even if you do not appreciate yourself at that moment. Otherwise, you might as well tell the person who gave the compliment, "I don't agree with you, and I can't allow you to feel that way." The absurdity, of course, is that the other person already *does* feel that way!

You might want to go a step further and examine why he or she gave you positive feedback. Perhaps you could learn to judge

---

TAKE ACTION

Do You Accept Compliments Well?

Some people can't accept it when a friend tells them that something about them is attractive or admirable. They actually disagree! "My dress isn't that pretty," or "My playing was awful, full of mistakes." You must learn to honor your friends' favorable perceptions of you. Try this exercise.

Ask friends and family to tell you something positive about yourself, something they like or respect about you. With a straight face, respond to the compliment by saying, "I'm sorry—I can't permit you to feel that way." If you can approach this exercise with some sense of humor, you may discover something important about how you unconsciously limit or even prevent compliments from coming your way. How can you feel good about yourself if you don't permit the kind of positive feedback that nurtures self-esteem?

yourself by the same standards. (How good would you feel if you were able to do that?) When you get a little more comfortable about accepting compliments, perhaps you'll learn to offer yourself some positive statements in recognition that you have done well. Eventually, as you become more experienced in accepting positive feedback from others as well as from yourself, you will see yourself more realistically (and less critically). Learn to recognize and use the strengths and abilities that were there all along and simply discounted by you. That is the key to developing personal power!

Be Careful of Where You Land
Jumping to Conclusions

A major error many people make—depressed or not—is to take a nugget of information and fill in around it with their own thoughts. The result: They reach a conclusion with few or any facts that objectively support the conclusion. Any time you form a conclusion, routinely ask yourself, "How do I know?" Your response should be more objective than "It's a feeling I have." The goal is to minimize such subjective thinking.

If you use yourself as the only frame of reference in trying to understand the actions of others, you must assume that other people think as you do. Likewise, you are insisting that others value what you value and take into account the things you take into account in deciding on a course of action. Using only your attitudes to relate to others means you are doomed to disappointment when they do not play the game of life according to your rules. The truth is, things that matter to you may not matter to them, and vice versa.

To avoid jumping to conclusions, you need to gather the information necessary for a rational decision. How do you know when you're properly prepared to suggest a specific course of action? In one common trap known as mind reading, people act as though they could see into the minds of others. Then they respond to what they presume the other person is thinking, never bothering to find out if they're right! This may take the form of getting angry with someone that you *think* is angry with you, perhaps because she is sitting quietly. Only later, after you're upset and depressed, does this person mention that she's been preoccupied with a problem that is totally unrelated to you!

Don't Chance It

You can't read other people's minds, even when you are *sure* you know what they're thinking. Why not ask the person to describe his thoughts so that you can see whether your assumptions are correct? Even if you are very sensitive and skilled in your relationships with others, even if you are correct 99 percent of the time, you might be way off this time! It is imperative for your own mental health to test your perceptions of reality by asking for feedback whenever it's available

In another form of jumping to conclusions, a depressed person forms an image of the future in which something goes wrong. The person suffers with all the negative and depressed feelings associated with that situation, even though it never happened! From other things I've mentioned in this book, it should be apparent to you how powerful your expectations are in influencing your experience.

If you create negative expectations, and you can't separate your mental images from the realistic possibilities in the situation, you're sure to face pain and depression. Therefore, I recommend that you learn to create positive images and sit in quiet relaxation, developing images and feelings associated with success. To do this, you should learn relevant techniques of self-hypnosis, meditation, and similar focusing methods. Sitting quietly and building expectations of success feels infinitely better than expecting the worst amid mental images of failure. It also serves as a mental rehearsal for carrying out the desired behavior later.

It's essential to stop jumping to conclusions when there's too little information if you want to avoid making obvious mistakes.

━━━━━━━━━━━━━━━━▶ **TAKE ACTION** ▶━━━

Can You Fill in the Facts?

Explain the reasons for the following:

▶ John drinks too much.

▶ John and Mary are getting a divorce.

▶ Mary was fired from her job.

▶ John's car was towed away.

▶ Mary did not get the raise she asked for.

Are you surprised at how easily you can create reasons for events you know nothing about? How does that relate to your experience of depression?

When you have a decision to make, or want to understand why something is happening as it is, gather all the information you can to get the most balanced and realistic view of that situation.

Mountains and Molehills
Magnification (Catastrophizing)
or Minimization (Trivializing)

Depressed people tend to exaggerate and focus on the negative things that happen and to minimize or discount positive things. It's a form of *dissociation,* another concept relevant to understanding your depression, that implies separation. You amplify one part of an experience, which separates it from other parts of the experience. Automatically, your awareness of the other parts is diminished. If I ask you to focus your attention on your right hand, in doing so you won't pay attention to your left foot (unless I mention it). If you focus on exterior sounds, you have less awareness of interior feelings. The term *selective attention* describes the fact that as we focus on *this*, there is less awareness of *that*.

Your conscious mind cannot pay attention to more than a couple of things at once. Therefore, what you choose to pay attention to says much about what you choose to ignore. In terms of magnifying or minimizing, if you focus internally on your feelings of failure in a performance, you miss the opportunity to realize that most of the audience liked what you did. By focusing on your negative interior views instead of the positive views coming from those around you, can you predict what your feelings will be?

Paying attention to what you consider a shortcoming prevents you from noticing that someone is simultaneously complimenting you on that same characteristic. Concentrating on the work you *have not* completed prevents you from simultaneously noticing how much you *have* finished. Highlighting the one thing you do not like about yourself prevents you from noticing, at the same time, anything you do like.

The goal is to push yourself toward a more balanced viewpoint instead of seeing things as black and white, good or bad.

➡ **TAKE ACTION** ➡

Find the Value in Facing Reality

Spend a full day forcing yourself to notice and respond only to the positive. Give lots of compliments to others, be patient and understanding—basically be syrupy sweet.

Are you aware of differences in your internal state? Name them. What does this suggest to you about being all-positive *or* all-negative? What does it take for you to be comfortable with the reality that everyone's life (including yours) has both positive and negative aspects? Explain how some negative things can happen without ruining everything.

You can see that by concentrating on one part, you virtually ignore other parts. Focusing on your feelings exaggerates them and minimizes your opportunity to read situations more clearly. Remember, there are times to get in touch with your feelings, and times to get *out* of touch with them.

Furthermore, if your feelings are consistently negative, you need external ways (such as feedback from others you trust) to evaluate yourself or your situation properly. The positive things you minimize and the negative things you maximize represent a considerable part of your depression.

Feelings Don't Make Sense
Emotional Reasoning

If you assume that your feelings reflect the way things really are, you set yourself up for a continuous flow of negative interpretations and distorted views that only reinforce your depressed feelings. If you say to yourself, "I feel that you don't like me, so I respond negatively to you," that's emotional reasoning. In other words, you are using your own subjective feelings to explain something rather than finding out what is really going on. You might never learn that the other person really is quite the opposite of what you thought.

Consider a person who needs romance in her life so urgently that she lets herself believe the man she is dating cares for her as much as she cares for him. After just a few dates, she's planning marriage, a family, and a life with him. But this scenario is only going on inside of her head, since the man has no intention of being committed to her in any serious way. He's a self-indulgent, opportunistic person who only wants a sex partner and will say almost anything to have one. If she had taken the time to learn this before she got caught up in her fantasies of marriage, she'd have realized that he was not marriage material. The preventive action against emotional reasoning that causes depression lies in learning to recognize realities by making sure things are as you think they are.

Human emotions are much too easily manipulated. Almost anyone's feelings can be guided toward a particular direction without too much trouble. And the reason is: *Feelings lie, feelings deceive.* What you *feel* is happening may have little or nothing to do with the true situation. Some people are skilled at making you feel a certain way to suit their own purposes. Television evangelists, for example, are expert at arousing guilty feelings or the fear of eternal damnation that gets you to send your dollars to God at *their* address.

The Manipulators

Hollywood is perhaps the best at engineering human emotions. In 90 to 120 minutes, filmmakers can create images and dialogue that move you up and down the emotional ladder. And what about salesmen? Have you ever been smooth-talked into buying a lemon of a car or some useless household appliance? How did the salesperson get you to buy? What motivation did she awake in you that made you buy? Obviously, at the time you bought it, you *felt* that the salesperson could be trusted and the product would be satisfying. If it was truly a lemon, you probably blamed yourself for having been influenced by an unscrupulous salesperson. You know firsthand how easily feelings can be manipulated. So you know that it's essential to consider other factors in addition to your feelings when making important decisions.

If you rely solely on your intuition (trust your guts) when you make important decisions, you leave yourself much too vulnerable to unconscious influences by people and situations. Feelings can lead you to make errors in judgment. I don't mean you should discount your feelings, especially since the message throughout this book has been to accept all parts of yourself as potentially helpful. The issue here is one of degree.

I am urging you to treat your feelings as *one* of many possible indicators for action and to look for facts outside yourself when-

---

LOOK DEEPER

Add Objectivity to Your Feelings

How do you know if you can trust someone?

How do you know if someone loves you?

How do you decide whether you can meet a challenge you want to attempt?

Do your responses reflect only your feelings, or do they include objective insights regarding the situation itself? What do you conclude about the validity of your answers?

---

ever possible. In my clinical experience, some of the biggest mistakes depressed individuals make come from responding to their own feelings (wishes, fantasies, expectations) without looking for some objective evidence that these feelings are based in reality. It's certainly true that your feelings are one element in deciding a course of action, but you must realize that they are the most subjective and arbitrary of all. Remember: *Feelings lie!* Whenever possible, use more objective criteria in making decisions.

Going for the Guilt
Should *Statements*

In the previous chapter I discussed the fact that an overdeveloped sense of responsibility is common among depressed individuals. It's what leads you to think things like "I *should* visit my mother, I *should* catch up on paperwork this weekend, I *should* clean the closets," and so forth. If you think in terms of all the internal *shoulds* and those that come at you from others, you know what a burden the *shoulds* are. It is up to you to decide

---

➡ **TAKE ACTION** ➡

Limit the *Shoulds* in Your Life

List things you should do in your life. What should your profession be? How should you spend your leisure time? How should you spend money? How should you feel about religion?

To all of these and to others *you* generate, add, "Who says?" Who knows what is better for you than you do? Why should anyone else have that power to dictate how you should be? How can you reclaim that power for use in your own best interest? When is it to your advantage to do what you should?

---

whether an expectation placed on you either by yourself or others is comfortable and realistic for you. To do that, you have to know and respect your own needs, so you can resist being pressured or bullied into mistakes.

The relationship between *should* and feelings of guilt, anger, and frustration is readily apparent. Go easy on the *shoulds* in your life. You can do this by establishing your own values (instead of accepting those of others), defining your own standards of success (rather than responding to ideas others have of what worthiness is), and becoming more realistic about what is and what is not an acceptable performance by you in some area that defines your positive self-image.

Who Are You?
Labeling and Mislabeling

By now you know that people label themselves or others, then respond to the label instead of the person. We do this because it frees us from the mental effort of recognizing distinctions and responding to individual differences. It is certainly much easier. A wonderful piece of research, done over 25 years ago, beautifully illustrates the problems that result from labeling others.

The Case of the Phony Patients

Psychologist David Rosenhan conducted an experiment in which normal graduate students and professional colleagues admitted themselves to various psychiatric hospitals. Each complained to the individual hospital admission staff that he was hearing a voice. The staff member assumed that a person complaining of hearing a voice and seeking admission to a psychiatric hospital must actually be crazy.

Once admitted, the bogus patients were to act entirely normal, waiting for the hospital staff to discover that they were not crazy at all. It took an average of 19 days for the subjects to be released! Other patients were quick to realize that these subjects were normal. They were curious to know if the subjects were journalists investigating the hospital or had some other hidden purpose in being there. The staff, on the other hand, interpreted nearly everything these interlopers did as pathological. If they took a nap, they were withdrawing; if they watched TV, they were escaping into fantasy. In other words, once they were labeled crazy, all their actions were seen in that light.

The experiment dramatically demonstrated a profound lesson for the mental health profession. It's essential for all of us to respond to the actual behavior and patterns of an individual, rather than affix a label on him that colors our response to everything he does.

The same point holds true for yourself. If you label yourself according to some experience you have, you lock in a self-perception that may be inaccurate and damaging. For example, if you label yourself a loser because your boyfriend breaks up with you, it shows an unchanging (stable) perception about your overall ability to relate to men, rather than a changeable (unstable) realization that this happened with only one particular

---

→ **TAKE ACTION** →

The Power of Labels in Defining People

List ten words in response to the question, "Who are you?" You may describe professional, social, intellectual, or other characteristics about yourself. What is the emotional tone associated with each word? Is it a label that makes you feel good, or is it hurtful in some way? Is the label fixed or changeable? How would you feel if it were negative and unchangeable? What labels do you attach to others of importance in your life? Do they work for or against the person? What would they have to do for you to drop that label?

---

man. In chapter 5, the stable/unstable discussion emphasized the fact that individuals who perceived their situation as unchangeable recovered from depression more slowly than others, if they recovered at all. It highlights the need for you to deal with things situation by situation, instead of generalizing with fixed labels. What about the label *depression*?

Why Is Everybody Talking about Me?
Personalization

If you go to a football game and worry that the players in the huddle may be talking about you, you're personalizing. You tend to think things that happen are personal when they're not. While the example is meant to be humorous, those who tend to personalize do see almost everything happening (in part or entirely) in relation to themselves. Suppose your department's budget is cut. You assume it is because your work is not valued; that's personalizing an event that may have no personal basis at all. As you already know, you must avoid jumping to a personalized conclusion before you have any objective information. If you pull yourself out of the emotional loop and attempt an objective view before you presume any harmful intent against you, you'll profit emotionally.

Ask before you react. Remember that others may make decisions you don't like, but they are not made just to hurt you. For example, your child's moving away from home to attend college is not a slap at you as a parent. Your child is growing up! Isn't that what you intended? People just do what they need to, and your job is to accept the choices they make as right *for them,* without taking it personally. Of course, if you learn that a person consistently makes selfish decisions that hurt you, it's a signal to expect less of that person. More discussion about such people appears in the next chapter.

SOME BASIC TRUTHS ABOUT FAULTY THINKING

The emphasis in addressing erroneous thinking is the need to gather objective evidence, to tolerate ambiguity when necessary, and to develop the ability to respond to situations and make decisions in ways that don't rely solely on your emotions. Depression distorts your perceptions, and distorted perceptions help cause depression.

As you begin to assert better control over yourself by addressing these interior issues, I want you to stop paying such close attention to your feelings, since you can see the many ways they may mislead you. Your feelings can and do deceive you. Important as feelings are, they are useful only so far as they allow you to respond effectively (inwardly and outwardly) to the flow of events in your life.

SOME BELIEFS CAN BRING YOU DOWN

Earlier in this chapter I focused on patterns associated with depressed thinking. Now I will present some of the most common beliefs that keep resurfacing among the depressed clients I work with. Wholesale acceptance of these beliefs can put you at risk for depression. I don't mean these beliefs are inherently wrong, but they're wrong enough *at times* to cause emotional harm.

I want to make it very clear that no truth operates equally well in all situations. Every situation must be judged on its own merits when you decide how to respond—or whether to respond at all. What was true in one situation may not be true in another. What was true yesterday may not be true today. What seemed reasonable before may be totally unreasonable now.

Unfortunately, the beliefs described in this section are casually tossed about on a cultural level as truisms, statements that *seem* so obviously true as to be beyond question. Not questioning these truisms may lead to emotional difficulty when you discover, painfully, that what you thought was true was not. Thus, in presenting each belief, I will comment briefly on its limitations. I hope to encourage some critical thinking on your part, so you can see when a particular belief system is likely to be helpful and when it might cause problems.

Where There's a Will, There's a Way?

If you reduce all problems to a simple question of motivation, where do other vital factors—physical possibility, emotional limitations, and costs—enter the picture? The suggestion that "you can do anything if you really want to" places a huge burden of personal responsibility for success on you. It eliminates every opportunity to question whether you are, in fact, personally responsible for (or even capable of) achieving this successful outcome. The net result of this belief system is an overwhelming sense of guilt if you fail.

From the discussion on control in the previous chapter, you know your will is not enough if success is beyond the realm of your control. For example, you may have an intense desire for your child to be the brilliant scientist who discovers the cure for

---

➡ TAKE ACTION ➡

Recognize What *Isn't* Possible for You

Can you recall an instance in which someone suggested that if you really had the will, you would have succeeded at something in which you failed? What was your reaction? Did you focus on feelings of failure and incompetence, or did you evaluate whether success was even possible?

Create a strategy to use when you need to evaluate the possibility of success *before* you invest your will in the project. Next, experiment with trying to motivate people to do impossible things: "Fly! Flap your arms and fly! If you really want to, you'll be able to!" What if you substitute "Heal yourself of cancer!" for "Fly!"?

---

cancer. But suppose the child prefers artistic over academic pursuits; the situation is beyond your control. There may be a will, but there is no way. Another child may have a strong will to discover the cure for cancer, but that's no guarantee that she will find it. Motivation is not the question; the necessary skills and resources, and whether the feat is humanly possible—those are the limiting factors. Many people have a will to live forever, an admirable desire, but the odds are stacked against success.

All Things Happen for a Reason?

The need to find a reason for the things that happen in your life is part of creating and maintaining the illusion of control. Reason implies that there is an order to things, an organized plan for the way things work out. The possibility that things happen in a random way is simply too threatening for some people. So they look for and find a reason for everything that happens, even if they have to make it up. In the absence of a logical, objective reason, they turn to faith.

> **LOOK DEEPER**
>
> ## Do Your Beliefs Enhance Your Life?
>
> Think about life experiences that are beyond explaining—babies that die or young people who lose a limb to disease. Why do these things happen? Does your view of such things help you or hurt you in other life situations? Does your belief have limits, or does it explain everything to your satisfaction? Would giving up your beliefs create too much doubt for you to tolerate? How do you know?

For many people, faith in some Divine Plan provides a comfort. However, others see it as an excuse for not learning how to manage life better. Faith helps to explain the unexplainable, and that makes some people feel better, but that puts them in the shaky position of trying to guess at God's intentions.

One woman I treated was in chronic pain as a result of being injured in a car accident. Immediately after she left the hospital, she began to look for some reason for the accident. She decided it was due to her personal flaws. Perhaps the accident happened because she was not at home where she *should* have been doing her cleaning. Or maybe if she'd been at her daughter's school program, as a good parent *should,* she wouldn't have been hit.

As she generated more reasons for the accident and what God's meaning could be, she became increasingly frustrated, anxious, and depressed. It was not in line with her belief system to consider that she was simply the victim of a random event. The accident was certainly bad enough, but her need to interpret it as happening for a reason simply made matters worse. Some events in life *are* random. That's why we call them accidents.

There Is One Right Way to Live?

Your society helps you set up a system for judging all your experiences. If you are taught to be intolerant of others who are different from you, to devalue their beliefs, customs, or worth, you can easily evolve an attitude that says, in essence, "My way is the right way; therefore, everyone else's way is wrong."

Every newspaper and TV report provides ample evidence of the many who insist that their way is the only way. Abusing or killing those who worship the wrong god or who have an opposing political viewpoint or different lifestyle is clear evidence of this distorted way of believing.

In depression, you may actually abuse yourself in this way. If you are uncomfortable with your own feelings and values, you may be your own worst critic for not living right.

What is the right way? It is obvious that despite the vast differences among the cultures of the world and among the individuals we know personally, very different approaches to life are quite successful. The goal is to develop the flexibility it takes to recognize that there are many right ways to live. The question is not "Is it right?" but "Does it work?"

When someone makes a career choice you do not like, spends

➡ **TAKE ACTION** ➡

Take Refusal in Stride

Attempt to convince at least ten people of the importance and rightness of a truly worthy social cause you are personally indifferent to. Talk to them about volunteering for the cause. What do you discover? How would you feel if you got those reactions about a cause truly important to you? Why is it that most people don't get involved in vital issues such as the environment, overpopulation, drug abuse, crime, and so forth?

If you do this exercise, you will learn a lot about how different the values people hold really are. And you will learn how each of us must live according to our own definition of personal integrity. But when someone refuses to get involved in or support something you consider important, you will be better prepared to accept it without feeling rejected.

money on things you do not value, or enjoys things you do not enjoy, it is his decision. The more you attempt to impose your beliefs on others, the more you discount their ability to make decisions for themselves. If they react negatively to your interference—and they will—your depression will increase. When others attempt to impose their idea of what's right on you, you must resist them with confidence that your way may be different from theirs, but it works for you. There are many ways to go through life. Just make sure yours works to *your* satisfaction.

JUDGE NOT, LEST YE BE JUDGED?

Many people are taught to accept everybody, disregarding any strengths or limitations in ability or character. They believe others can do anything they want to do—the old "Where there's a will, there's a way" phenomenon again.

One woman believes that if she's sexy enough, her husband will not cheat. That's emotional reasoning. In fact, this woman can't make accurate judgments about the man she is involved with. Assuming that being sexy will prevent her husband from straying doesn't consider the right question: "Is this man capable of making a commitment to me?" As she sees it, her desirability governs his commitment. So his degree of loyalty is up to her. Obviously, this man may be one who simply does not value commitment or loyalty, and he may have no intention of being faithful to her, no matter what she does. Meanwhile, she will keep trying and get increasingly frustrated and depressed because she can't get what she wants from him. She will go on blaming herself, never recognizing that the limitation lies in the man!

To have a satisfying relationship, it's essential to judge your intended partner to determine whether he or she can and will provide what you want. Yet I am often struck by how blindly some of my clients entered into relationships with others. The reason is quite clear. The mechanism of emotional reasoning

━━━━━━━━━━━━━━━━ ➡ **TAKE ACTION** ➡━━

Practice Evaluating Others Objectively

Prepare a list of important things you would like to know about someone new—things to give you a sense that you really know her, not events but values, desires, and lifestyle patterns. Go out of your way to meet three new people in a social context. How can you get such information from them, casually, without seeming to conduct an interrogation? How do you interpret the responses you get so you can judge the person's capabilities? Hopefully, you're responding to facts and patterns, *not* just your feelings.

permits the person to feel that this loved one can develop what's missing (such as sobriety or the motivation to achieve). But the person doesn't go beyond the feeling to find out whether this loved one wants to—or can! While it is important to know what you want from another, it is imperative to know whether others can and will provide it.

You Are Responsible for All Things That Happen in Your Life?

I hope this belief system was dismantled in the previous chapter. Examine it and identify the truth about where responsibility falls in each individual situation. It is virtually *impossible* for you to be responsible for *all* the things that happen in your life. Others exert an influence upon you, and that influence is inescapable. Don't succumb to the wishful thinking that the right attitude or approach will let you make anything happen. The converse is equally true. It is debilitating to believe that if yours is the wrong attitude, all the worst things will happen to you. Your internal world plays a huge role in what you experience,

---

➡ **TAKE ACTION** ➡

Learn to Refuse Unreasonable Responsibility

Imagine you have something like the stock market, the weather, or the price of oranges to be responsible for. How do you feel about paying attention to and being tied to something you cannot control or answer for? What if you really believed you were responsible?

---

but the reality of the world around you also has a significant impact.

You Must Solve Your Own Problems?

Many depressed individuals trap themselves in the distorted idea that any changes in life are entirely up to them. Remember, you did not develop your view of the world all by yourself. Many people were instrumental in shaping your experiences, ideas, and values. To believe that new learning and new experiences, particularly relative to your problems, must come entirely from within places you at an extreme disadvantage. You now know

---

Examine Your Tolerance Level   ↳ **LOOK DEEPER** ⌐

Can another person's opinion be of value when you feel stuck with a problem? Can you recall a time when you felt stuck and someone said or did something that helped? When should a person seek therapy? How much pain should you tolerate before seeing a doctor or dentist? How and when will you know it is time to seek outside help? Will you wait for things to reach crisis proportions?

---

how distorted a depressed person's thinking can be, so it's obvious that relying only on your own thinking may block out more realistic ways of looking at things. Just as you did not develop the attitudes that cause your problems all by yourself, you must accept that the ways to solve problems may also come from outside of yourself.

A Commitment Must Always Be Honored?

The ability to make meaningful commitments to other people is the cornerstone on which any society is built. To be as good as your word is a trait valued universally. Others build their trust on the basis of your ability to deliver on a promise. Yet there are times when circumstances demand that you alter or break a commitment you made.

Perhaps the most familiar example of such a development is divorce. Most couples marry in an atmosphere of love, lust, and a desire to be together always. Adjusting to the reality of marriage—sharing daily experiences, deciding on mutual goals, and dealing with the stresses of living together—can result in growth experiences that distance the partners from each other. Situations may arise that drive a wedge between the partners. If this happens

➡️ **TAKE ACTION** ➡️

Know When to Walk Away

How do you know when to walk away from a negative situation? What about "If at first you don't succeed, try, try again"? List examples of life situations where a commitment can be honorably broken. Should a wife stay married to her husband on Death Row? Should a parent support an adult offspring who is capable of independence? When should agreements be renegotiated? Can a reevaluation point be built into the original agreement, anticipating that circumstances might change?

to you, should you sacrifice your own mental health and potential for happiness to honor a previous commitment? Or should you recognize that the circumstances in which the commitment was made have changed to the point where it is detrimental, even destructive, to maintain the commitment?

This difficult choice is faced by millions of Americans yearly. If they divorce, are they bad people who could not honor a commitment? Not at all. They have painfully and responsibly faced the reality that something once worthwhile has become destructive.

Each individual must decide for himself when it's the right time to let go of a painful situation. But you must define that time clearly, knowing you have done everything possible to evaluate and improve the situation. In my experience, it's a mistake to let go before then. There is nothing worse than having doubts later: "Did I do everything that I could have done? Perhaps if I had . . ." Such follow-up self-recriminations fuel guilt and feelings of depression.

There Is One Best Solution to a Problem?

Just as there is no one right way to live, there is no one way to address the problems you face in your life. Consider this book as an example. In the very first chapter, I described a number of different ways to look at and deal with depression. Each way works, and that's why I included them. It is not a question of which one always works best; the question is, *Which one works best for a given individual in a given circumstance?*

Sometimes the best solution is clearly identifiable; at other times, a variety of viable solutions are equally acceptable. In some ways, it is like being asked which is the best car to buy. Best for what—speed, looks, reliability? The goal is to evolve a broader framework for problem-solving. Life continually poses new problems for us to respond to. The more effective you are at using different approaches to problem-solving, the more likely

━━━━━━━━━━━━━━━━━━━━━ ➤ **TAKE ACTION** ➤━━

You Decide What's Best

Choose a task that seems relatively straightforward, like buying a car, and ask a number of your friends, "What is the best procedure for choosing a new car?" Which of the strategies offered sound efficient, and which sound like a setup for buying a lemon? Did the respondents ask for clarification ("What are you looking for in a car?"), or did they automatically give you their personalized strategies, assuming that you are the same as they are? What do you conclude about solutions to a problem?

you are to succeed in a wider number of situations. Generating solutions means finding things to do that work. The underlying practical, commonsense philosophy is: If it works, don't fix it; if it doesn't work, do something else!

Your approach to solving a problem will not be identical to someone else's approach to the same problem. Yet both of you may be equally capable of generating a good result. Here is another opportunity to demonstrate some flexibility. You may be working with a colleague on a joint project that requires problem-solving. You come up with a solution you know would work, but so does your colleague. You may both be right, even though you have two very different types of solutions. Problems often have multiple solutions, and it will be to your emotional advantage to allow for that possibility.

If You Are Fair, You Will Be Treated Fairly?

This is a spinoff of the Golden Rule all of us learn as young children. Unfortunately, not everyone subscribes to the Golden Rule. Many individuals have a very different set of morals and ethics from you; some do not even feel a twinge of guilt as they

---

═══▶ **TAKE ACTION** ▶

Whom Should You Trust?

Ask at least a dozen people: "Have you ever been treated unfairly by someone you thought would treat you well? What happened and why? In retrospect, could you have known the probable outcome of the situation, or was it totally unpredictable?" What patterns do you see emerging in the responses? What role does blind faith play in the responses? What does it suggest to you about the value of gathering information about someone *before* getting very involved?

---

deliberately take advantage of or hurt another person. The belief that you should not be judgmental or critical of others places you at an extreme disadvantage.

Some people have no sense of fair play and respond only to their selfish interests, regardless of who might get hurt. I don't want you to develop a streak of paranoia, but I do want you to rely less on your own feelings and think more about the nature of the person you're dealing with. This is especially true of a personal or romantic relationship.

Learning as much as possible about someone you want to be involved with is necessary for determining realistically how much of yourself you can share with this individual. Learn to be selective in your self-disclosures until you know if the other person can respect and appreciate what you have to share. There is a marked difference between *paranoid* and *cautious*. Learning about another person slowly and deliberately is an effective way to develop a realistic sense of this relationship's future. If you want patience and understanding in a partner, you don't want to discover, only after you have made a commitment, that both are lacking. Think preventively.

Your Feelings Are the Most Important Part of You?

How frequently do you hear that psychotherapists encourage their clients to "get in touch with your feelings"? Having previously discussed the unfortunate tendency to be guided by your feelings, we know their value as an indicator for action is questionable. Those mental health professionals who say feelings are the highest form of awareness have to deal with the limitations of that viewpoint. If it's true (and I believe it is) that feelings deceive, and depressed feelings are decidedly distorted toward the negative, why place the highest value on the awareness of feelings? Clearly, using feelings that might be distorted and negative as guidelines for what to do places you at serious risk. It should be obvious by now that feelings are hardly the most important part of an individual. They may sometimes be the *least* important center of focus simply because they can delay, even prevent, an effective response to a situation. Again, the goal is to be selective about when to focus on your feelings and when to shift the focus away from them.

LOOK DEEPER

When Feelings Don't Work in Your Favor

Identify accomplishments in your life that were achieved independent of your day-to-day feelings. For example, how did you manage to go to class, write papers, and study for exams for four years in college, even though there were many times you would rather have been doing *anything* but schoolwork? How did you keep going with your education, in spite of the many times when you felt like quitting? What inner resources permitted that? How might those same resources serve you well in other areas of your life? Think of any specific accomplishment that took you a long time to complete. How did you stay with the goal despite varying levels of interest and energy?

KEY POINTS TO REMEMBER

- What you think and how you think are the key factors in creating and maintaining depression.
- You can easily identify some common errors in thinking that fuel depression.
- All-or-none thinking is the tendency to interpret your experiences in extreme ways.
- When you make one experience represent an entire class of experiences, you are overgeneralizing.
- In using the mental filter mechanism, you focus on one aspect of experience to the exclusion of all other relevant details.
- If you tend to reject positive input from others by devaluing its worth or somehow ignoring its significance, you are disqualifying the positive.
- If you take a small piece of information and fill in missing data with your own subjective thoughts, reaching a conclusion not justified by the facts, you're jumping to conclusions.
- When you exaggerate the negative or minimize positive things that happen in your life, you're inviting depression.
- When the basis for interpreting experiences is your feelings, and you assume that they actually reflect reality, you're using emotional reasoning.

It is apparent that most of your experience is determined by your attitudes and your patterns of thinking. For that reason, I have encouraged you (through the "Look Deeper" and "Take Action" exercises) to challenge your own subjectivity by finding objective evidence whenever possible. Every pattern of thought and every belief system discussed in this chapter will be true or useful someplace, and each will be false and detrimental someplace else. Your task is to master these principles so that you can apply them effortlessly, situation by situation, to your own advantage.

- Too many *should* statements suggest overresponsibility, leading to guilt, shame, and self-criticism.

- The tendency to attach a name or idea to an experience and respond to the name instead of the experience is called labeling and mislabeling. It's difficult to develop any sort of positive regard for yourself if you label yourself negatively.

- You're personalizing if you take impersonal things to heart.

- Depression distorts your perceptions, and that helps perpetuate depression.

- Belief systems are patterned ways of thinking about and perceiving yourself and others. But these belief systems may lead to depression when they do not represent reality accurately. Few beliefs, if any, hold true in all circumstances; thus, the goal is to respond to each situation effectively on its own merits.

- Learning to monitor and correct your own thoughts and beliefs is essential for defeating depression and preventing future episodes.

Chapter 9

FIND OUT WHAT TO DO WHEN OTHER PEOPLE ARE A SOURCE OF PAIN

If you are depressed, certain relationship patterns may be particularly troublesome for you. To protect yourself against future distress, it's important to take an active role in directing your relationships. To help you do so, I will discuss some of the basic problem issues, particularly control and responsibility. Confusion over these two factors is not only potentially hurtful to you as a person but dangerous to your relationships as well.

Obviously, positive and healthy interactions with others are vital to your overall sense of well-being. But we know that such relationships don't just happen. In fact, they require a variety of important skills. Unfortunately, these skills seem to be on the decline in America. The high rate of divorce is just one of many indicators that this is so.

WHY WE HAVE TROUBLE RELATING

I believe that a primary reason for the decline in relationship skills is that we so seldom interact meaningfully with each other. We can do so much on our own that there is practically no need for contact with others. The corner grocer who knew you from years of shopping at his store has been replaced by a huge supermarket. If you died in an aisle there, the manager might not know it for days! The same goes for the old neighborhood gas station where the mechanic knew you from years of buying gas there; now you walk up to a mirrored window and ask the invisible cashier for "ten dollars on number four." It's like placing a bet!

You can see how quick and anonymous most of our contacts are. As a result, many people have no real connection with others at all. More people in this country live alone than ever before. Some are happy about that, but many are not.

No wonder there's a decline in relationship skills. As the emphasis on technology increases, so does the emphasis on individual capabilities. For example, the average American watches over four hours of television a day. (That's the time you'd spend on a part-time job!) But watching television cuts back on interaction even more. In fact, if other people are in the same room with you, TV takes your attention away from them.

Television certainly does *not* contribute to your communication skills, nor does it encourage you to understand your family and friends better. Add the television-watching time to the time many people spend in front of a computer screen at work, and you see why the need and desire to interact with others decreases over time.

The more hours you spend alone with television, the fewer you have to deal with other people on a casual basis. As this state of affairs escalates, an even greater need for deeper, more meaningful relationships may arise. Realistically, you can't create instant friendships, much less deeper intimacies. So any urgency you feel to make too much happen too fast is a ticket to trouble.

THE QUICK FIX FIASCO

The divorce rate in America exceeds 50 percent; the average dating relationship lasts only several weeks. This reflects a quick

---

Review Your Style of Anger　　　↳ **LOOK DEEPER**

Often it's the people we love who provoke us to anger most. They know how to press our button. They also are the ones most easily and deeply hurt when we lash out insensitively.

What do you say or do when you are angry with people you care about? Do your words or actions threaten their security or indicate a willingness to deal with problems realistically, with respect for the value and the integrity of the other person?

---

fix mentality—to feel good, solve problems fast, or avoid them altogether (all-or-none, remember?)—that leads to a very low tolerance for frustration. It says you have a need to overcome the problem quickly, even if the resolution is a Band-Aid that is only temporarily effective. Such thinking makes it likely that the couple will move on instead of reasonably addressing any problem that should arise in the relationship.

Unfortunately, the throwaway society we live in also includes marriages and families, so it is very hard to develop a sense of security. How can it be otherwise when the threat of losing the entire relationship is continually present? For that reason, each person must be especially careful not to threaten the other person's sense of security if the relationship is to work. When you have the urge to storm out of the house angrily, but you stay and address the issues instead, it's a strong positive message to your partner. If the impulse is to hurt the other person by trying to make her feel afraid or jealous, but you put your arms around her instead, the message of caring is powerful.

Each individual has many needs that can only be satisfied in the context of a close personal relationship. When those needs for emotional support, intimacy, and the expression of sexuality are not met, the sense of urgency to satisfy them is amplified. This need for speed *increases* the likelihood of making a mistake

What Are You Looking For?   ➔ LOOK DEEPER

To get what you want from a relationship, your partner must be in on what you're seeking. The only way that can happen is if you state your needs explicitly. What does the phrase *your needs* mean to you? How would you define your needs in a relationship?

by starting a relationship with someone who is simply not able or willing to give what you want.

DEFINING YOUR ROLE IN A RELATIONSHIP

In the earliest stages of life, our roles in society are based solely on gender: Here's what a girl does; here is what a boy does. Those roles are created by the same society that shapes you to fit them. In the process, you establish expectations for your own behavior as well as the behavior of others.

By custom, the woman is socialized to be other-oriented. She is conditioned to be highly sensitive to others, ready to accept a secondary role built around their needs. Is it any wonder that women frequently feel unfulfilled? Is it a coincidence that women are diagnosed as depressed twice as frequently as men?

Traditionally, males are socialized to be competitive and achievement-oriented. That helps to explain why historically, men are far more susceptible to stress-related illnesses than women. (However, it is significant that as traditional sex roles change, blurring the lines that separate the genders, the incidence of stress-related illnesses in women is going up!) The cultural emphasis on men as achievers may explain (not excuse) why some men seem to have trouble developing intimate relationship skills.

→ **LOOK DEEPER**

Playing the Part

We all know what men do and what women do in our culture. These traditions were taught to us very early, but society has changed. Do you fit the sex role stereotype? If so, to what extent? How were you raised to fit this stereotype? If you don't fit your sex role, how did you learn to buck the stereotype?

The important point about being assigned a role is that every role brings with it a set of expectations. An individual's performance (competence in a role) is judged by how well those expectations are fulfilled.

When you bought this book, you expected that it would teach you how to deal effectively with depression. Suppose the direction of the book had changed after the first few paragraphs. Suppose the bulk of the book dealt with investing money instead of handling depression. Your original expectations for the book would have been unfulfilled, and you probably would have had a negative reaction to it. The role of this book is to address depression. To the extent that it does so, your expectations are met and you have a positive feeling about it.

In relationships, you have expectations, too. After all, the chief benefit of being in a relationship is that your partner will provide certain dimensions of experience you can't provide for yourself.

HOW TO RATE YOUR EXPECTATIONS

Are your expectations realistic, too high, too low, or irrelevant? If they are based on what you want, rather than on what the other person has to give, they are unrealistic and can only

---

➤➤ **TAKE ACTION** ➤

Your Personal Benefits Plan

What things do you expect a relationship to provide for you that you cannot provide for yourself? List these things, and notice whether the words you use are concrete (physical contact) or abstract (emotional support). Define in very clear and practical terms what you mean by any abstract words or phrases you listed. Then list specific things your partner could do to provide these things.

---

set you up to be disappointed. Unfortunately, it's hard to know if your expectations are inappropriate. Sometimes you have to learn through the pain of disappointment when they are not met. And when you face the reason, it may be more hurtful than the disappointment you felt.

To ease the pain, you may blame the hostile, unpredictable and unmanageable world, thereby assuming the position of helpless victim. Or you may heap the blame upon yourself, concluding that you are unworthy of having your needs met. That response reinforces a poor self-image and builds more expectations of personal failure and rejection. Obviously, your interpretation of events is important in influencing how you feel and what you do.

Some individuals try to avoid disappointment by stifling all expectations. To dismiss the value of having expectations in one broad sweep shows the distorted thinking of overgeneralization. It's an unrealistic way of managing yourself. You need to have *some* expectations in your relationships. You must be able to make appropriate demands on others (note the deliberate use of the word *demands*) as part of maintaining a healthy give-and-take. The expectations must represent a good fit between your needs and the other person's ability to meet them. Of course, the reverse applies as well.

A MARRIAGE IN DANGER

Let me illustrate by telling you about my client, a very nice man named Jack, also a therapist. He and Jane, a graduate student currently completing her doctoral degree, have been married for two years. Jane is highly ambitious and deeply absorbed in her education and career. By putting project after project ahead of time spent with Jack, she makes it clear to Jack that although she loves him, he is less important to her than her career. Jane assumes that he will quietly and willingly adjust to her professional goals and hectic pace.

When Jack expresses disappointment over her last-minute cancellations of their plans, or when he wants her attention so he can share his interests or life burdens with her, Jane is usually irritated with him for distracting her. Sometimes she even angrily accuses Jack of being too needy or of trying to make her feel guilty about her pursuits, thus attempting to sabotage her efforts. As a result, Jack has learned to express no disappointment, share no problems, and avoid talking to Jane about his deeper needs or his dissatisfaction with their relationship.

Jack feels trapped and helpless. He has little hope that things will ever improve, yet he desperately wants them to. He has become increasingly depressed and withdrawn.

As a therapist, Jack knew the signs that indicated it was time to seek help before things got too far out of hand. He knew he was hurting; he knew what he wanted, but he did not know what to do about it. He felt like a victim of his marriage, and depression was the result.

The unbalanced relationship was painful to both partners. In such situations (where the partners have different and seemingly opposite goals), you are likely to find at least one partner depressed. In this case, I want you to notice how gaps in expectations surface as depression. What mattered most to Jack—his marriage—did not seem to matter as much to Jane. Jack was unable to manage effectively what mattered to him the most, and he felt victimized and hopeless as a result.

SEARCHING FOR THE ANSWER

What abilities was Jack missing in his relationship with Jane? Would better communication skills have helped? What if Jack could skillfully turn Jane's defensive or angry reactions to him in a positive direction for establishing new relationship goals? Suppose Jack had other supportive relationships, so that meeting all his needs didn't fall solely on Jane? Would it help if Jack could recognize Jane's situation as nearing an end, because she would be through with school soon?

All these things and more could have and, in fact, *did* help Jack. Instead of feeling like a victim, he adjusted his expectations to a better acceptance of Jane's life choices. In exchange, Jane committed to follow through on plans she made with Jack and agreed to make herself more available to him on a regular basis. Their relationship was solid enough and loving enough to permit those readjustments. Jack stopped expecting all of Jane's attention, as he had originally intended. As a result, Jane found Jack less needy and more enjoyable to be around. That increased her interest in being with him.

It's clear from this story that sometimes less is more. Jane's career ambitions did not diminish, but she gradually spent more time with Jack. She communicated to him in a variety of ways that he was the most important person in her life. Once Jack knew that, and once he stopped personalizing her career choices, the relationship improved dramatically.

Can one partner meet all the needs of the other? Probably not. It's better to realize that a variety of needs can be met in a variety of ways. You and your partner must decide which needs are best met within the relationship and which are best met elsewhere. For true intimacy to evolve, each partner's security and well-being must be protected. The proper attitude is that the well-being of the relationship is more important than any specific problem. The ideal is "*us* against the *problem*," not "*you* against *me*."

KNOW YOUR PERSONAL NEEDS

It is difficult to have your needs met if you don't know what they are. Think about the things you require from a relationship: honesty, security, love, passion, monogamy, fun. . . . *Recognize* them and *accept* them as basic parts of who you are; let it be known that they are important. The things you value are correct for you, and you are entitled to have them.

Or course, the fact that you want those things doesn't mean that your partner will want them, too. Relationships tend to take the most negative turns when things one partner values are devalued or ignored by the other. Recognizing your needs as legitimate establishes a framework of self-acceptance; then you can take the healthy position that those needs should be acknowledged and responded to by your partner.

But it's your job to provide a "user's manual" that will teach your partner about you, your inner world, and your way of dealing with things, so he or she can relate to you in the most positive and effective way. That's why dating is so valuable—it provides the opportunity to learn about another before you invest a lot of emotional capital in that person.

To minimize your own needs by focusing on those of the other person is a strategy for failure. Vital and healthy relation-

---

➡ **TAKE ACTION** ➡

Instructions for Using You Right

What will it take to make you most productive, most loving, most amusing, most content? You should be prepared to tell your partner these things.

Pretend that you are a product someone has just purchased. He opens the box and finds a user's manual attached to you. What will the manual say? Write a guide to the best use and best care of you.

ships require a high degree of shared responsibility and sensitivity. The strategy is to have *both* partners give in order to get.

THE MESSAGE IN THE MARTYR ROLE

If you place yourself in the role of rescuer or martyr, you deny yourself, making your partner (or family member) your primary focus. In one way or another, you are stating that the other person is worth more than you. It's hard to feel valuable in a relationship built on acknowledging the greater worth of the other person.

One form of martyr role frequently associated with depression is the tendency to protect others from your depression. Now this pattern is not entirely lacking in sensibility, since most depressed individuals learn soon enough that others don't want to know about all their personal problems or hear their complaints. However, in an intimate relationship, holding back your true

---

LOOK DEEPER

Share to Clarify Thinking

It is fine to be discreet about how much you share regarding your depressed feelings. We know that not everybody wants to hear every psychological pang you suffer. However, there is no merit to holding it all back from those who love you. Telling the right people about your feelings and concerns may bring you some help through the new views they offer.

Can you see how keeping distorted thoughts to yourself limits your opportunities for change and improvement? What does that suggest to you about the importance of learning other perspectives to free yourself from depression?

feelings interferes with closeness and prevents you from getting other perspectives on life that might clarify your own thinking.

CASTING YOURSELF AS THE VICTIM

Assuming the role of victim is another mechanism for denying your own needs. By assuming this helpless posture, you show that you can't assert your needs, so you can't build a relationship in which your needs must be considered. You virtually ask to be taken for granted or otherwise mistreated. When you place too few demands on the other person concerning your needs, you're saying, "My feelings do not need to be recognized and respected by you." By assuming the victim's role, you unwittingly train your partner to disregard you!

Your awareness and acceptance of your needs is your recognition and affirmation of your individuality. You're not *asking* if it's all right to want these things or need these things. You're stating that you want and need these things, and this is how you expect to be treated. You should know that it's essential to be aware of the *specific* conditions under which you are at your best, so you can communicate that to others. Simply put, you are responsible for asserting your preferences, feelings, and needs. But bear in mind that just communicating what you want doesn't mean you'll get it. Your partner may be unable or unwilling to respond. That's why it is so important to know your partner's capacity for meeting your needs.

TECHNIQUES FOR ASSESSING OTHERS

How do you know if you can trust someone? Are there *specific* criteria you can use? If you answer some variation of "I trust my gut feelings," you are using the distorted thinking known as emotional reasoning which I discussed in chapter 8. If you think you can rely solely on your intuition, you are responding to you, not to the other person.

By focusing on your gut feelings and other internal states, you could miss external information that might elicit fresh reactions or new choices. It is precisely this type of internal absorption that limits your ability to read and handle situations effectively, and it often results in depression. As a simple example, consider the way some people behave upon being introduced. They are so self-absorbed, wondering "Am I okay? Do I look okay?" that their internal preoccupation impairs their ability to pay attention to the new acquaintance. No wonder that they can't remember the name even a second later.

You simply cannot be effective in dealing with others if you are too internally focused. Instead, it is important as a general strategy to focus externally when getting to know someone new. Specifically, observe the other person's attributes, values, and patterns so you can quickly develop a strong sense of this individual and his style. The best attitude to take when meeting someone new is to assume that you're okay; then the task is to find out whether he or she is.

GUIDELINES FOR CHOOSING A PARTNER

It may sound cold and clinical to assess others, but it's essential to know what matters to another person and what he or she is capable of in determining the course of your future relationship. You need guidelines for understanding who this other person really is and what type of relationship you might expect to have together. Being disappointed or hurt by others is a common theme among my clients. It shows me how frequently they misread the people they get involved with—usually seeing them as they'd like them to be, not as they really are.

Control. Does this person attempt to impose her standards and values on you, or does she accept you as you are? If you feel pressure from this person that suggests you should somehow

━━━━━━━━━━━━━ ➡ **TAKE ACTION** ➡ ━━━━━

Sizing Up Somebody New

When you meet someone for the first time, what are the traits on which you form an impression of that person? Write the names of some people you've met in the last month. Next to each name, jot down your general impression of him or her. In a third column, describe *specifically* what this person said or did to warrant that judgment from you.

be different than you are, be aware that she is attempting to make you see things or do things her way. The message she's sending is that you're not okay. The more she tells you you're not okay unless you do it her way, the more you feel hurt and inadequate.

Deciding to keep that person around, even though she tells you you're lacking, is choosing to stay in an environment that might eventually harm your sense of well-being. The healthiest way for two people to live together is for each to recognize their differences and accept them, rather than use them as ammunition against each other.

Responsibility. Does this person accept responsibility for himself, or does he consistently blame others for the problems in his life? For example, suppose you are a single woman out on a first date. Eventually, you ask the man, "Have you ever been married?" He replies, "Yes. In fact, I've been married three times." When you ask what happened to his marriages, he responds, "Well, my first wife was an alcoholic and she was intolerable. My second wife ran around with other men, and my third wife was a gold digger who was only after my money."

If you meet a guy like this and you start to feel sorry for him because he's been so unlucky in love, my advice is to *run the other way!* A man who explains his three divorces in terms of "blame, blame, blame" is not a good risk as a partner. Nowhere does he accept any responsibility for choosing those he married, nor does he acknowledge any of his own contributions to these breakups. If you have to be around such a person (at work, for instance), keep things safe and superficial between you. Don't expect him or her to be a responsible person unless you see evidence to the contrary.

In much of the relationship counseling I do, the imbalance that first leads a client into conflict and then into therapy revolves around the issue of responsibility. One partner wants to address issues; the other does not. One wants to blame the other for problems; the other is often all too quick to accept the blame. Responsibility in *any* relationship is a shared phenomenon. No matter how bright or strong you may be, you are only half of any partnership with another.

Problem-solving capabilities. Does this individual face problems directly and demonstrate an ability to work through them, or does he deny problems or attempt to run away from them? Like life, every relationship has problems. The fact that the problems are there highlights the need to have two people facing the issues jointly and realistically. When one partner wants to solve problems and the other only wants to have fun, the imbalance that results may eventually ruin the relationship.

Depressed individuals in particular tend to focus on problems to the exclusion of fun and relaxation. Before you label your partner as less than competent in dealing with problems, try to evaluate yourself realistically. Are you busy creating the gloom and doom that the other person in the relationship is trying to escape?

Communication skills. Is your partner able to express his or her feelings, needs, and views? Or is this person so close-mouthed that you're uncertain and insecure about the best way for you two to relate? Some people find it hard to express their feelings. They simply do not have the depth and awareness it takes to communicate their innermost being.

It's common for the woman in a relationship to continually press the man to express himself, *assuming* that he is holding back on what he really feels and thinks. In fact, he may be exactly as he appears, not holding back *anything*. What she sees is what she gets! Some wag once said, "If you take a walk through the ocean of most people's souls, you will barely get your feet wet." It's simply incorrect to assume that everyone has profound feelings or thoughts. Some people are remarkably superficial. Before you push for depth and openness, look for evidence that it's there! It could be that there are no hidden gems in there, and to assume otherwise is hazardous.

Consistency. Do your partner's actions match what she says, or is there a gap between the two? Remember the concept of cognitive dissonance, in which the need to keep things the same permits distortions in your own self-image. It was discussed before, primarily in terms of forming a negative impression and dismissing feedback on that basis. It is fair to say that the self-image of *most* people is distorted to one degree or another. If someone tells you, "I am a sensitive individual," he is telling you how he sees himself. That self-disclosure says *nothing* about what the person really is. The sensitive person might turn out to be quite abusive. No one is likely to say, "Hi. I'm mean and I'm insensitive, and I treat my dates very badly." To respond only to what someone says is to miss the more significant dimension of what that person *does*.

If you feel a sense of urgency to get deeply involved with someone quickly, you are far more likely to respond to that person's words simply because you haven't had time to find out if his actions match his talk. That is why I place a *huge* emphasis on taking your time in getting to know someone, so you can see first-hand the degree of consistency between what he says and what he does.

There is a phenomenon social psychologists call the "honeymoon effect," the tendency to share your best in early meetings in order to make a good impression. So when you begin to establish a relationship with someone, particularly a romantic one, be aware that you're seeing that person's best qualities. No arguments, sarcasm, criticism, or inconsiderateness surfaces in those earliest encounters unless those traits are too strong to control. However, most people have enough finesse to hold such negatives in check until they feel safely established in the relationship. There is simply no substitute for taking time to get to know someone by experiencing them under a variety of conditions—socially, with your friends, his friends, and your respective families, and alone, in all types of situations. Only through such experiences over a significant period can you develop some assurance about the way this person treats you and the way he responds to the ongoing demands of life.

BUILDING A HEALTHY RELATIONSHIP

Notice the word *building* in this heading. It is intended to emphasize that a healthy relationship does not just happen. The magical images Hollywood creates for us in romantic movies and on television are not real life. People don't just ride off into the sunset to share a trouble-free life together.

➡ TAKE ACTION ➡

Rate the Influence of Others

Every person who is important in your life leaves an impression that helps to make you what you are, for better or for worse. Name at least a dozen people in your life who have been significant influences in your development. On a scale of 1 to 10, how does each of those individuals rate on each of the five patterns—control, responsibility, problem-solving, communication, and consistency—just described in this section?

What was the impact of their strengths and weaknesses on your development? How does their lifestyle affect your relationship with them? What characteristics do their patterns encourage in you? Do you like yourself more or less as a result?

It takes a great deal of purposeful guidance from the very beginning to move a relationship in a progressive and positive direction. At the outset, the aim must be simply to establish healthy patterns of relating. If you view yourself as actively guiding a relationship, you must be sure you are not in a depressive victim role—passive, helpless—for that would place you at great risk for steering the relationship off course, perhaps to the point of self-destruction.

DOES LIKE ATTRACT LIKE?

As a general rule, optimists don't hang around pessimists. People who are not depressed, who are having a good time in life without a lot of problems, find the negative aura that surrounds depressed individuals a drain. Whom do you want to attract into your life, and why? You have to think about the kind of relationships you want to have so you can determine which parts of yourself to share and when. Should you build a relationship on negativity, a need for sympathy, a need to have someone to hear your complaints? Hardly a good way to start. A relationship established on such a basis means you have two negative individuals reinforcing some of the worst patterns in each other.

When you have two depressed people together swapping stories of pain and anguish, you have the blind leading the blind. I'm not discounting the value of having someone to support you during difficult times. I am suggesting that a relationship established solely on shared negativity and complaints creates a framework that contains its own seeds for destruction.

It is best to build a relationship with a positive future in mind. After all, depression won't always be there. Having a mutual goal of sharing good times together—and expending effort to do so—allows the relationship to develop in a more balanced and positive way. I encounter many couples who start out in the midst of personal crisis—teetering job, failed marriage,

---

▶ **TAKE ACTION** ▶

Are You Having Any Fun?

Make a list of at least a dozen things you like to do to relax and have fun. Next to each activity on your list, note whether you like to do it alone or with others. Identify those activities that require planning and those that require money. Then note the last time you did that activity. Keep this list handy for when you feel down and need to do something to feel better. Build lots of play into your life to counterbalance your problems.

---

financial reversal—and they do very well in commiserating together, but they don't know how to have fun together. Of course, the ability to solve problems is important, but having fun must be among the priorities, too, just for a sense of balance. By paying no attention to the need for good times and leisure, many depressed couples reinforce each other's depression. They emphasize a deep exploration of important issues that creates a draining aura of intensity around the relationship. Balance comes from spending time together on superficial endeavors that have no deeper meaning than enjoyment. My advice: Dare to be superficial! Dare to be silly sometimes, instead of forever hashing out the deep intricacies of life.

Depressed individuals are often intolerant of experiences they see as superficial and useless. Such a value system makes them want to get right to the deeper feelings of others. This is a bad strategy, as you will see in the next section.

THE ART OF SELF-DISCLOSURE

How do you know how much to reveal about yourself, or when and to whom? Is it best to be an open book or secretive and withholding in relation to others? The answer depends on the outcome you want. If what you want is to find a sympathetic ear or a sounding board, then going through life telling people all your problems is likely to bring you a steady supply of rescuers. But a relationship established on that basis automatically sets up a victim/rescuer situation, reinforcing negative roles for each.

You must learn to self-disclose selectively, at a pace that matches the other person's self-disclosures and that is reasonable for the context. Don't share deep, personal information before the relationship is strong enough to support the weight of such disclosures, or it might collapse. If it does, the confider may feel abused, misunderstood, trivialized, and definitely depressed. Hopes and expectations fall apart because of the attempt to introduce too much too soon!

At a party, you meet someone and you put out some light conversation, such as "Hey, how about this weather we're having?" Your brand new acquaintance answers, "Yeah, the weather's been weird . . . and I'm really broke, I think my kids are on drugs, and I'm on the verge of a nervous breakdown, and . . ." Now you know how uncomfortable an imbalance is. You want superficiality, but this person wants to make you his best friend in your first three minutes together.

An urgency to make a relationship happen leads to mistakes in the weight and quality of your self-disclosure. The solution: Go easy! Learn about the other person's ability to relate, to speak of personal matters, to accept, and so forth. The idea is to disclose at a rate that gradually adds depth to the relationship. The key word is *gradually*. You can't create an instant best friend; it takes time—even if she has the potential to be a great friend. The process requires patience to let the relationship grow.

The desire to add depth to a relationship gradually is certainly worthwhile. But not everybody's capable of a deep relationship. If weeks, months, or years of regular contact go by with no growth of intimacy, there may not be any more for him or her to give. Do *not* assume that this person has greater depth and is simply not sharing it with you for some negative reason. Be careful not to jump to conclusions or personalize the actions of such individuals.

The ideal is to be with someone who can appreciate you and accept you for who you are. Learn gradually whether this person accepts you as you self-disclose, or whether you sense negative judgments and messages that say this person feels you're not okay and really should be different.

With each new disclosure, you risk being rejected. That is precisely the reason for sharing only selected parts of yourself at a gradual pace. Be careful not to let threats of rejection by others control you. Likewise, be careful not to invest yourself in someone who lets you control him. Give-and-take in relatively equal proportion is the essence of healthy relationships.

IT'S VITAL TO SET LIMITS

Building a relationship means establishing rules for conducting the transactions between the parties. But rules are useless if they are not clearly stated and enforced. Setting down and enforcing such rules is known as setting limits. The inability to effectively set limits on others is the mark of a victim mentality and makes such a person an easy target for the manipulations of others.

It is human nature to want what you want when you want it. The question is, How far will a person go to get what he wants? There is a range of tactics or manipulations you can use to get your heart's desire. The chief problem with being manipulative is that, while it may get you what you want from the other person, it devalues that person.

In essence you're saying, "My getting what I want is more important than your feelings." So such tactics work against the long-term health of a relationship by hurting the self-esteem of the other person. Think of your own experience. If anyone has

---

→ **LOOK DEEPER**

Do You Encourage Manipulations?

Think of the last three times that you felt manipulated by someone. What was the tactic he used? How did you feel about yourself for having been manipulated? Why did the manipulation work? Does this sort of tactic work with you consistently? If so, you can recognize how you helped train this person to be a manipulator by not setting and enforcing limits.

---

ever laid a guilt trip on you, you know that you not only felt guilty, but you were angry, too, that anyone would cause you to feel that way.

The seven most common manipulative tactics are guilt, intimidation, withdrawal, seduction, flattery, fast-talking logic, and sympathy ploys. Each of these tactics may work, but only as long as the other person permits them to. For example, if you use the tactic of intimidation (by throwing a tantrum, yelling, or threatening violence), people may give in to you, but considerable resentment and, eventually, rebellion is generated in the process.

DEALING WITH A DATE WHO'S LATE

Here's an everyday scenario: A man asks a woman for a date, and she accepts. He says he will pick her up at 8:00 P.M., but he does not show up until 8:45. The woman faces a decision: Does she ignore his being late because she does not wish to appear confrontational and risk his not asking her out again? Or does she make an issue of his being late, letting him know she was irritated at his lack of consideration? Well, if she says nothing, she is really saying she will accept lateness. If she speaks up about his lateness, she lets him know she considers her time as valuable as his.

It's not a question of whether she should let him know she needs to have her time respected—clearly, she should—but *how* she communicates that need. A straight attack strategy is effective only if she never wants the guy to ask her out again. Better: "In the future, I hope you'll take my time into account and call if you're going to be late." This is an appropriate assertion of her need to have her time respected. If he gets angry at her polite assertion, he's making a statement that says, "Anything that I do should be okay," which really means, "My needs come before yours." Establishing a relationship with someone who is self-centered and insensitive is a poor risk. It's better to know about him at the outset than to find out after she invests time and energy in him.

To help yourself with setting limits, the best thing is to ask yourself, "What am I communicating to this person if I do not establish and enforce a limit?" If you intend to let others know they can disregard important parts of you, then by all means, be passive and say nothing. On the other hand, if you want to be respected and acknowledged as important, then it is your responsibility to assert what is and what is not acceptable to you.

When the limits you establish are violated, it can only make

TAKE ACTION

Learn to Dodge Opportunists

Make a point of watching several of the television preachers on Sunday morning. Since their obvious goal is to raise money, it's clear what is wanted of you. Make a list of the tactics (guilt, fear, sympathy) they use to get you to part with your money. What specific phrases and demeanor are used in applying the particular tactic?

you feel abused and devalued. If you don't enforce limits (or even establish them in the first place), and you get manipulated as a result, you will probably be angry with yourself for not having done so. Furthermore, you will likely be angry with those who manipulated you for their personal gain while disregarding your needs.

Much of the anger commonly found in depressed individuals is due to their perception of being victimized. But anger vanishes when you establish and enforce limits that interrupt the cycle of abuses you once allowed. There is a decidedly better way to manage your anger than to pound a pillow in frustration.

IT'S ALL UP TO YOU

Do not expect others to protect you. It is your job to protect yourself. Other people will always try to get what they want from you, whether it's money, time, support, expertise, or your body. You must define your own limits and enforce them. It's totally unrealistic to expect others to do that for you. It's imperative that you not give others the power to determine your self-image.

When you say no to others, they may be inconvenienced or even hurt at not getting what they want. That doesn't make you wrong! As they stand there expressing disappointment or even anger to you, you'll feel guilty and upset if you become internally focused on having to say no and being the target of someone else's anger. Don't back down and give in, or you'll be violating your own limits, and you probably won't like yourself very much later.

The whole point is that evolving self-respect calls for setting clear limits and enforcing them in a manner consistent with your needs. Anytime the limits you set stop others from getting what they want, you can expect some negative feedback. Learn to tolerate it as the only way to enforce the limits you set. The approval of others should be incidental to your doing things in a way that makes sense to you.

MOTIVES OTHERS HAVE
FOR MANIPULATING YOU

If you learn to recognize other people's motives in using manipulative tactics, you will have a greater sense of freedom in dealing with their demands. Ask yourself why this person is trying to manipulate you: what he wants from you and why he is willing to make you feel bad to get it. What does this say about that person and his or her perception of you? When you can identify the manipulative tactics other people use, you'll see the need to *be firm* at all times.

KEY POINTS TO REMEMBER

- Healthy relationships don't just happen. Good relationships require very specific skills.

- Unless you practice your relationship skills, their effectiveness declines.

- Technology can discourage meaningful contact with others. For example, spending a great deal of time watching television limits your opportunities for interaction.

- Caring about another person means being willing to protect that person's sense of security.

- Our ideas about relationships come from our socialization, when we learned as youths how to fulfill the various roles of our lives.

- While it is important to have expectations about the way others will relate to you, it is essential to determine whether they have the capacity to meet your expectations.

- You are responsible for showing others the best way to relate to you. Remember, they are not mind readers.

- You must assess the ability of others to meet your needs, just as they must assess your ability to meet theirs.

- Do not judge others solely in terms of how they make you feel. Instead, learn how the person deals with these issues: control, responsibility, problem-solving, communication, and consistency.

Relationships built on the basis of acceptance and respect do not eliminate manipulation. Even if others love you and respect you, they still want what they want, so the threat of manipulation is ever present. The fact that others attempt to manipulate you is not the problem; the problem is whether you permit the manipulation to succeed by not setting and enforcing limits the other person can respect and accept. Respecting another person's right to choose precludes imposing your needs or desires on him to his detriment.

- It takes time to get to know someone well. Limit any sense of urgency you have to get attached to others, so you can be more objective about the people you get involved with.

- Like attracts like. Attaching to another depressed person and building a relationship on negativity may feel comfortable initially but eventually may prove problematic.

- Self-disclosure is an art. The rate of self-disclosure is determined by the rate at which the other person does it and by what is reasonable for the context.

- Setting down and enforcing clearly defined rules is known as setting limits. This is one of the most important mechanisms for building a strong and healthy relationship.

- To one degree or another, all people use tactics of manipulation to get what they want. It's your job to recognize and handle those tactics with self-protection in mind. The most common of these are guilt, intimidation, withdrawal, seduction, flattery, fast-talking logic, and sympathy ploys.

- The anger common to depressed people usually arises from the perception of being victimized. You can dissipate this anger quickly when you establish and enforce limits.

- Relationships are just one part of your life. Do not make your entire self-image dependent on them. You can't control others.

PUTTING IT TOGETHER

Learning the skills presented in this chapter will undoubtedly lead you to develop better, more satisfying relationships, which are a good source of comfort in life. However, relationships are just one part of your life. If your entire self-esteem or sense of well-being rests on them, then too much of yourself rests on factors that are not entirely in your control.

Up to now, you may have thought that good relationships result from chemistry or some other vague factor. In fact, the discussion in this chapter shows that good relationships have some very specific components. They don't just happen. Rather, like most things in life, success comes from taking definite steps to establish healthy patterns of relating.

➡ TAKE ACTION ➡

Dare to See Yourself as Others See You

What tactics do *you* use to get what you want from others—sympathy ploys, guilt trips, withdrawal, intimidation? If you feel courageous, ask the people closest to you for their observations on how you go about getting what you want from them. Then ask how they feel about the way you treat them. Perhaps you'll hear things you may not like, but they may help you move to a higher level of integrity in your relationships.

Chapter 10

INVESTIGATE WHEN AND HOW TO GET PROFESSIONAL HELP

Even though this is a practical self-help book, it would be unrealistic to think it could ease depression in *everyone* who reads it. Even if your depression persists after you have read the book carefully and experimented faithfully with the exercises, it doesn't mean that your problem is hopeless. However, it is a sign that your type of depression lies beyond the scope of this book and that it's time to seek professional help. We know now that depression is neither necessary nor inevitable, but it does need to be approached from an angle that *works*. The right professional will be able to help you discover what that angle is.

We all live inside our individual frames of reference, and most people find it hard to step back from their usual viewpoints to develop a fresh attitude about themselves or their lives. That's why it may be especially difficult for you to be objective enough to uncover new and better ways of responding to old feelings or situations.

I include this chapter on seeking professional help for three very important reasons.

1 Only a minority of the depressed individuals who may need it actually seek professional treatment. The attitude that says

"Why bother? Nothing is going to help" has been challenged repeatedly in this book. Professional treatment can work and work well, but you'll never know that if you don't even give it a try.

2 While it is true that the mental health profession is stymied in dealing with many psychological problems, depression is *not* one of them. The profession knows a great deal about depression and its effective treatment, so the success rate is very high. You really *can* expect positive results when you put yourself in the hands of a competent professional.

3 Many individuals who consider seeking help are so overwhelmed by the task of finding a therapist that they give up before they even get started (recognize the global thinking?).

My aim is to provide you with the basic knowledge you need to obtain competent professional help for yourself (or the depressed person you care about). I will also give you specific tools you can use to "shop" for a therapist.

WHEN TO GET HELP

For many people, the question of *when* to get professional help is the major concern. Here are six basic factors to consider in deciding whether to seek professional treatment.

1. Suicidal thoughts or feelings. Do you find yourself thinking about death frequently or fantasizing about the relief it would bring from emotional distress? These are definitely suicidal thoughts. If the thoughts are vivid, meaning detailed to the point of specific ways to kill yourself and the chain of events that would be triggered by your death, there is even more reason for concern. You need immediate therapeutic attention.

Suicide has been called the permanent solution to a temporary problem. The belief that your future holds nothing but more pain is distorted, depressed thinking. Suicidal feelings and thoughts need to be dealt with professionally, as quickly as possible.

2. Acute depression turning chronic. Sometimes depression comes on rapidly after a traumatic event (for example, the death of a loved one, the breakup of an important relationship, the loss of a job, or a severe illness or accident). Though painful in the short run, this type of depression can be considered a normal response to difficult circumstances. Most people return to their ordinary level of functioning following a brief and hurtful episode of depression. Some few, however, never seem to bounce back completely.

If you feel that your depression is lasting longer than it should, it's time to get a professional opinion for peace of mind. Also, if you find yourself making negative decisions during this depression period that might stick for a lifetime ("I'll never be happy again"), it's important to get some objective feedback.

3. Lifestyle disruption. When your depression becomes so severe that it impairs your ability to function well in various areas of your life, it is essential that you seek help before life situations deteriorate to the point of no return. Ending your marriage, losing your job, or abusing your body and physical health due to an episode of depression will likely lead to even more depression later. Take steps to prevent the downward spiral from causing you still more pain.

4. Reality testing. If you are in a position of relative isolation and there's no one you can talk with about your thoughts and feelings, you have no way to get a reality test. That is, you have no way to check out your perceptions with others who have a more objective viewpoint. Considering all the distorted thinking patterns described in this book, it should be obvious that speaking with a more objective party can be extremely valuable in getting you back on a realistic track. A therapist can be the partner you need for reality testing.

5. Inability to help yourself. It may be beyond your capabilities to step outside your own (depressing) framework of reality and help yourself effectively. Often someone outside your frame of reference, such as a therapist, can provide input and feedback that is refreshingly beyond anything you would have been able to generate yourself. A new pair of eyes on your problems may lead to fresh solutions. Furthermore, a caring relationship such as that in good therapy has healing qualities that go far beyond what you can experience on your own. (And if relationship problems are a lot of what goes on in your life, how can you solve them *by yourself?*)

6. Extreme nature of symptoms. Many of depression's symptoms exist on a physiological level (see Bill's story in chapter 2). If you are severely depressed—unable to eat or sleep well, unable to concentrate well enough to learn effectively, and have no energy—you may benefit from more immediate interventions, such as antidepressant medications. They may help you become more receptive to the additional benefits of psychotherapy. Continuing to put up with such extreme and unpleasant symptoms is delaying unnecessarily the important positive changes that can be made with the right kind of help.

Once you have made the decision to seek professional treatment, you are faced with finding a competent professional. Start here.

APPROACHES TO TREATMENT

It is little wonder that the public is confused by the intricacies of the mental health field. There are so many categories of mental health professionals—psychiatrists; psychologists; marriage, family, and child therapists; pastoral counselors; lay counselors; social workers. Each has a different title and educational background, with a distinct way of looking at problems like depression. How can you know which is the best therapist for you?

We can divide the mental health field into two general areas: biological and psychological. True, they do overlap, but their differences are exaggerated here as a way to clarify some points. Bear in mind that these approaches are *not* necessarily mutually exclusive in terms of treatment.

Drugs as the Basic Treatment

The one and only practitioner in the biological realm is the psychiatrist. He is an M.D. who specializes in the diagnosis and treatment of psychological disturbances according to a particular medical system. Psychiatrists take advanced training, using psychoactive medications (drugs that affect the mind) and physically based treatment for handling psychological disturbances. They also learn psychotherapy techniques to complement the use of medications.

In treating depression, the psychiatrist's primary tool is antidepressant medication. In a case of depression so severe that the person is literally unable to function, the treatment may be more intensive, including hospitalization and perhaps electroconvulsive treatment (ECT). Commonly known as shock treatment, ECT has been the subject of fear and horror stories, but to many clinicians and researchers, it is the treatment of choice for severe depression. However, it should only be used in the most extreme cases. In fact, psychiatrists manage the overwhelming majority of their depressed patients through the use of antidepressant medications.

These medications have repeatedly shown their effectiveness in providing relief from the symptoms of depression. Most depressed individuals experience relatively rapid relief when antidepressant medications are correctly prescribed and taken, although nobody understands exactly how they work. So if your depression is highly disruptive to your life and you experience very uncomfortable symptoms, particularly on a physiological level, consider consulting a psychiatrist concerning the appropriate use of antidepressant medication.

Of course, there are certain concerns in using antidepressant medications. While they may provide marked symptom relief (usually in less than a month), these medications do not change your way of explaining life events or your way of thinking or relating to others. So the potential for recurring depression remains unless you receive additional psychotherapy along with the antidepressants. The medications also have side effects that may be a source of discomfort until you adjust to them. But that is a minor consideration for most people.

One final point: I am concerned about how the medications may discourage your active participation in changing the depression-causing patterns. Using medications alone can unwittingly encourage you to be passive when it is critical that you actively learn new and healthy lifestyle patterns.

For these reasons, I am cautious about encouraging the use of antidepressants unless the symptoms are severe. When indicated, I prefer to use hypnosis and other stress-reducing, attention-absorbing processes. I am being deliberate, though, in pointing out to you that antidepressant medications are effective, especially when combined with other therapy techniques.

Psychological Approaches to Treatment

Psychotherapists assume that whatever psychological or emotional disturbance you have is a product of your experience— the things you learned and the things you didn't learn as you matured. The psychological approach primarily involves *talk therapy,* that is, exchanging ideas, perspectives, and philosophies between therapist and client. This book is psychologically oriented, encouraging you to consider the ways you think about and relate to the different aspects of your life.

Any practitioner whose approach to treatment involves your learning new views and skills is providing psychotherapy. This term covers literally dozens of types of treatment, each with its own assumptions and approaches. Since the typical depressed individual does not know one approach from another, he may get confused when trying to choose the *best* therapy. In fact, there is no *best* therapy. If you think of therapy as a detailed confession and endless talk about your mother's mistakes with you as you grew up, your impression is a common one, but it is inaccurate. Treatment has many different approaches, and it is important for you to find out what to expect from each type of practitioner.

I want to suggest in a general way that the type of therapy you seek for depression is of great importance in your eventual recovery. Even more important is the nature and skill of the therapist you work with. Throughout this book, I have emphasized my lifestyle prototype of depression. I have also stressed the basic thought processes and the interpersonal actions that have consistently shown their effectiveness in the treatment of depression. Psychotherapists of all levels and backgrounds (psychiatrists, psychologists, social workers, and the like) are trained in these approaches. The academic degree of the professional may be important to you if you equate level of education with expertise. I believe a more advanced or specialized degree is no guarantee that the therapist can apply the specific principles of therapy efficiently, and after all, that's the most important criterion. In saying this, I am openly suggesting to you that professional skill, more than an academic degree, determines how effectively therapy is conducted.

FINDING THE RIGHT THERAPIST

Unfortunately, just when you need to expend energy "shopping" for a therapist, you are least motivated and energized. Finding a good therapist is not easy. You need to ask many questions, take various factors into account, and consider many possibilities. Therapy for depression can usually be completed in less than 20 sessions, and I believe that it's unnecessary to provide endless details about your unhappy past. Focusing on hurt, anger, or any other negative feeling can amplify your depression and still not teach any new skills or correct any erroneous thinking. Therefore, it is reasonable to ask potential therapists for specifics on how they would treat your depression.

A referral from your family physician is a good place to start. Just know that many physicians have an exclusively medical or biological viewpoint and are likely to recommend a psychiatrist. You may raise the subject with friends or relatives you trust who have had experience with therapy. If you're new to your city, the phone book might be your only reference source; check the yellow pages for *Psychiatrists, Psychologists,* or *Counselors,* and call a few. Feel free to ask for basic information about academic degree, state license status, their usual approach in treating depressed patients, and the average length of treatment. It is unreasonable to expect an extended conversation about your case on the telephone, but it is fair to expect enough of the therapist's time to get basic information.

You can ask about the fee per session, health insurance coverage, how your progress in therapy will be evaluated, the frequency of the sessions, and when the therapist is available for regular appointments.

If you are satisfied with the information provided, you can schedule a first appointment. At that time, you can expect to describe your experience of depression, including your symptoms, your ideas on what your depression is about, and what you have already done in attempting to get over it. During this first session, you should also get an idea of how you relate to the therapist and whether he or she will provide the support, feedback, direction, and structured learning activities you need.

YOUR THERAPIST MUST CONVEY HIS SUPPORT

Keep in mind that while you are intelligently evaluating your potential relationship with the therapist, cognitive distortions and negative interpersonal patterns that may characterize depression can creep into this situation. It is important that you stay aware of your need to set limits and avoid emotional reasoning, jumping to conclusions, and personalizing on the basis of the feedback that you get from your therapist. If your response to this person is negative, or if you feel the level of expertise you see is not up to your needs, it is not only desirable but *necessary* for you to move on. Do not allow yourself to be manipulated by a therapist who attempts to convince you that your depression is to blame for any lack of empathy between the two of you. You *must* feel valued, supported, and positively challenged to grow by your therapist if the treatment is to succeed.

A therapeutic relationship is a special one, yet it embodies many of the same principles other positive and healthy relationships have. Think of your therapist as an educator, not a substitute parent. The therapy relationship must have the same expectations of receiving acceptance and respect that you would want in any other relationship. And it is imperative that you set clear limits in this relationship.

The therapist's expertise in an area of vital interest to you is no basis for having your needs or views discounted. You are an essential half of that relationship. No one knows your experience, background, and thoughts better than you. In that sense, you are the expert on you. It is your job to educate the therapist about who you are and how you do things, so he can get a clear sense of where best to intervene. If the therapist repeatedly goes off on subjects you find irrelevant or unnecessarily hurtful, you should say so.

The therapy relationship is confidential, so whatever you say about yourself must be kept in the strictest confidence, both by law and by professional code. Only two exceptions allow the confidence to be broken: threatening harm to yourself or another person, and abusing a child. Thus, virtually nothing you say will ever go beyond the therapist. His skill provides a secure environment that permits you to explore your distorted perceptions, depressing beliefs, and self-limiting patterns. If he is good at teaching you more effective lifestyle patterns, the likelihood of your recovery is very strong.

HELP TO SHAPE YOUR TREATMENT

It bears repeating that you are an important half of the therapy relationship. It is imperative that you take an active role in shaping the direction of the treatment, even though you may

KEY POINTS TO REMEMBER

- Each person's experience of depression is unique; therefore, if your experience of depression lies beyond the scope of this book, you are well advised to seek professional help.

- The mental health profession knows a great deal about depression and its effective treatment, so the success rate of treatment is very high.

- There are six basic factors to consider in deciding whether to seek professional treatment.
  1 Suicidal thoughts or feelings
  2 When short-term depression starts to become long-term
  3 When the depression starts to disrupt your lifestyle
  4 When you have no one with whom you can test out your view of reality
  5 When you have reached an impasse in your ability to help yourself
  6 When the nature of your symptoms is so extreme that it becomes difficult for you to function

- Treatment generally takes the form of biological and/or psychological intervention.

- Most experts agree that the best treatment for depression involves using some combination of antidepressant medications and psychotherapy.

- The use of antidepressant medication alone is generally not a good idea.

- In the majority of instances, psychotherapy for depression can be completed in a brief therapy format involving from 1 to 20 sessions.

- It is imperative that you choose a therapist knowledgeable in the nature of depression and both long- and short-term methods of treatment.

- It is your responsibility to be an intelligent consumer, to gather and weigh information about potential therapists.

not know exactly what things you need to learn or how to learn them. It must be understood that therapy is not something *you do* or is done *to you,* but a process in which *you participate.* Your input and your willingness to disclose and to carry out well-intentioned therapeutic assignments are vital to the process. It is a great paradox of therapy that even the best therapist can help only to the extent that the client allows help.

Remember, therapies are as subjective as the therapists who practice them. If you go for therapy and the experience is not beneficial after a reasonable time, do not overgeneralize about the negative quality of all therapy or personalize in a way that says it works for everyone but you. Use the explicit criteria in this chapter as a checklist for being a smart consumer of therapy services. With persistence and awareness of your own needs concerning the approaches you might respond to best, I have no doubt that you will find the quality mental health professional you want.

Epilogue
GETTING ON WITH YOUR LIFE

Now you can limit the painful, depressive episodes in your life by using what you've learned about the nature of depression and its treatment. You know that life's continual challenges make each of us vulnerable to the pain of depression when important things go wrong, or worse, when catastrophe strikes. An obvious first step in coping with this is to recognize the warning signs of trouble that require your attention.

RISK FACTORS FOR DEPRESSION

Just as cigarette smoking puts people at risk for eventually developing lung cancer, we know that certain risk factors pave the way for depression. *Any* pattern that reflects an imbalance in important areas of your life is such a risk factor. This condition results when you are unable to find the necessary resources within yourself for coping with the demands you face, whether they come from others or from within yourself. Generally, any pattern that leads to a one-size-fits-all approach to life is risky.

Because of its automatic (unconscious) nature, each type of

erroneous thinking (cognitive distortion) described in chapter 8 can surface at any moment, leading you to experience pain. The challenge lies in learning to recognize and correct the cognitive distortions associated with depression before they can take hold. You have the opportunity to work at that nearly every moment.

Your explanatory (attributional) style also presents a significant set of risk factors. As discussed in chapter 5, to the extent that you form attributions that are internal ("I'm the one"), stable ("It will always be this way"), and global ("It affects my whole life"), you risk personalizing things that are not personal and assuming things will stay hurtful forever and have a negative effect on everything you attempt to do.

The degree of your personal rigidity is a risk factor. The core of mental health lies in the ability to shape your experience and create new experiences for yourself, rather than passively allowing events to shape you. You will never outgrow the need to recognize *quickly* when it is time to do something else and to act *flexibly*. The more you automatically dismiss ideas or experiences that conflict with your beliefs, and the more you prevent others from sharing your thoughts and feelings (which means they can't question them), the more you will be working to maintain your discomfort level.

Life continually presents opportunities to seek and experience new things, and each new experience gives us a chance to develop new inner resources. It is these internal resources (ability to take risks, develop new skills, solve problems, and so forth) that we must effectively draw upon to meet life's demands.

THINGS *NOT* TO DO

Throughout this book, I have deliberately emphasized activities you can do to help yourself. I don't believe in telling people what *not* to do, since it does little to create new courses for action. However, I will violate my own principle here (see how flexible I can be!) with a list of things *not* to do if you want to defeat depression. As you read these, I hope you will use the earlier discussions of each as reminders to refresh your memory.

Do not dwell on the past. It's over, and history can't be changed. What matters is tomorrow and all of your tomorrows. Make changes *now*, so things will be better *later*. See how to overcome things you learned in the past that were either wrong or ineffective.

Do not compare yourself to others. You are unique, trite as that may sound, and measuring yourself against others distracts you from the more immediate tasks—identifying specific experiences *you* need to have and skills *you* need to learn to move forward with *your* life. There will always be people a little better and a little worse than you; the most important task you have is to develop yourself as fully as possible.

Do not create and dwell on negative possibilities. Sure, it can be good to anticipate potential snags in your plans, but the larger picture should emphasize the useful things to do, not the negatives to be avoided. The idea that "Obstacles are what you see when you take your eyes off the goal" is the right one.

Do not leave important things unsaid or undefined. It is necessary to bring the abstract into reality and define global thoughts more completely in everyday living. Save the abstract philosophies about the meaning of life for discussions that are not directly involved with your well-being. The things that directly impact your feelings about yourself—your relationships, your health, your job, and such—are the things that should be well defined and managed.

Do not reject basic parts of yourself. Each part of you is valuable somewhere, sometime. Rather than try to rid yourself of parts you have labeled bad, learn to acknowledge the presence of those parts and the circumstances in which they can actually work to your advantage. For example, anger is not bad; it's a basic and necessary emotion. But throwing tantrums is not an effective way to deal with anger. When you learn when and how to express anger (as well as your other feelings) appropriately, you will have a valuable skill that helps you to stay healthy.

Do not ignore your own needs. As you know, depression often comes about when your inner world becomes unbalanced because you invest excessively in other people and in external situations (such as promotions at work). Balancing your needs against the needs of others is vital for good mental health.

Do not ignore reality in order to follow your own desires. If you focus on your own wishes without regard to realities of the current situation, you will respond ineffectively to what's going on in your world.

Do not give up. To expend effort and fail is certainly painful. But let me remind you that most things you want to do are probably doable. The deciding factor is the strategy (series of steps) you follow to achieve your goal. If you try something and fail, don't just try harder doing the same thing, *do something else!* If you know others have done it, that means it can be done. If you can't figure out how to do it, get someone else to show you how. If you fail, it reflects less on your capability than on the way you went about the task. It is vital that you continue to expend focused effort intelligently. When you don't know what to do, the effective move is to get help, not to give up.

Do not leave time unstructured. Depending on how you use it, time can be your greatest ally. Actively structure your time to bring out your best. If you feel good when you are out in nature, get out there as much as you can. Build your schedule to include leisure activity along with your work, relaxing time with others and time alone, physical rest along with physical exertion, and so forth.

Do not stop working on yourself when your depression lifts. You are aware that you can be at risk for depression even when you are not depressed. Continually monitor your attributions, thoughts, relationships, and perceptions of control and responsibility as your best means to prevent recurrences. If you have too much difficulty identifying in yourself the patterns that get you down, make use of professional help. If you are in therapy and it's working, stay until all concerns are resolved.

THINGS TO DO

I hope all the ideas and techniques that are presented in this book provide you with many useful paths to follow toward self-discovery. Unlike a novel that is read once for the story it tells, this book has so many different possibilities that I urge you to use it continually for the exercises and ideas that help you push yourself toward new understanding and competence.

I have four final pieces of advice.

1. Be aware that you can't prevent stressful things from happening in your life. Of course, stressful experiences are the most likely precursors of depression. However, you can manage stress by thinking ahead, learning to relax, and stepping outside the urgency of the situation. These are important skills for maintaining your balance and for recovering quickly when shaken.

2. You must develop effective problem-solving skills if you are to manage your life effectively. Dealing with what is, instead of just fantasizing about how things can or should be, is the necessary starting place.

3. Emphasize self-awareness, particularly in the areas of your personal needs and values. It is essential to behave in a way that is consistent with your needs and values.

4. You need to build your life around factors within your control whenever possible. This is particularly critical if you are prone to depression. Be especially careful of people or things you get attached to or depend upon. If you tend to be victimized easily or assume too much control, any situation in which you make an emotional investment is potentially hazardous. Caution.

Depression is no longer the mystery it once was. As you learn more about your internal world and how it functions when you deal with the external world, you will develop more and better ways to respond to life situations. At times it may not seem this way, but you really do have the power to choose. I hope you will use that power for a future of satisfying growth and purposeful change.

INDEX